eMolecule

eMolecule

HARNESSING YOUR
ENTREPRENEURIAL SPIRIT

—

MARY TODD

DISTINCT PRESS

Book Cover Design: Susan Veach
Cover Photograph: Stephen Orsillo

Summary: Everyone has an entrepreneurial spirit (an "eMolecule") and through self-exploration to find your passion, you can enterprise your passion through business to create a more fulfilling life so you can live your purpose.

1. Business & Money : Women & Business 2. Self-Help : Communication & Social Skills 3. Biographies & Memoirs : Leaders & Notable People : Social Activists

---

Library of Congress Cataloging-in-Publication Data
2015930314

Todd, Mary 1983 -
eMolecule: Harnessing Your Entrepreneurial Spirit

PRINT VERSION ISBN-10:0991608992
PRINT VERSION ISBN-13:978-0-9916089-9-7

Printed in the United States of America
10 9 8 7 6 5 4 3 2 1

To everyone out there with the eMolecule,
To all who have shaped my life,
especially my husband, Geoffrey,
who is truly the most amazing person I know.

DISTINCT PRESS PUBLISHING

If you are interested in bulk ordering of paperback versions of this book,
please contact us directly at ordering@GTomniMedia.com.

If you are interested in professional review copies of this book because you intend to
write a review in your publication, mention this book on your radio show or podcast,
post to your blog or website, or request an article or interview, send your request to
reviewcopy@GTomniMedia.com.

For more information visit

www.eMaryTodd.com

10% of proceeds from the sales of this book are donated Africa Yoga Project.

CONTENTS

PART THREE

AUTHOR'S NOTE

I can honestly say that I am amazed each and every day that people whom I don't even know, and also those who I *do* know, have so much faith in my ability to deliver. It was not until I started down this path that I would begin to recognize this. Either something had shifted in me or I was now more aware: more aware of myself and more aware of my surroundings. I have certainly become more confident.

I have spent my fair share of days, nights, and moments curled up in the corner with tears fueled by fear and self-doubt streaming down my face. It still happens from time to time. Not because I am weak, but because life seems hard, really hard, and sometimes, we all just need to cry. But I have learned that no matter how bad it seems, really it is just *me*, judging myself and creating *my* own set of problems and expectations, making me feel scared and second-guessing my decisions. But guess what? It is also *me* who picks myself back up, dusts myself off, and sends me back out into the world to experience another day. Before we get started on this journey together, you should know three things about me.

First, I <u>love</u> food. I love cooking it, eating it, experiencing it. I love it so much that I once started a food blog because I thought it would be a relaxing outlet for me to express myself. It was a failed project because I learned rather quickly that I actually don't like *all* things about food. Food photography is awful and tedious, for me at least. I just don't have the willpower to pour over lighting and perfectly arranged garnishes after completing a dish.

I slobber more than a Pavlov dog trying to take those tantalizing photos. Oh yeah, and my inability to actually write down the ingredients or the specific measurements of what I put into my dishes made recipe creation virtually impossible. Cooking takes place *in the moment.* Garlic and chili flakes sautéing in hot oil will not stop and wait for me to position and take a photograph or write down accurate measurements or record the exact timing. I believe cooking is a bit like having a sixth sense that you can coax out with enough practice. I don't know how long that simmering garlic or those chili flakes will take to release their flavor; I just know it's ready when I see it and smell it. Hence the reason why my food blogging adventure was a horrible failure.

Second, I am a nerd. Seriously. I read the dictionary during the summer between third and fourth grade. It turns out my two favorite words of all time are muttonchops and ignes fatui. Who knew muttonchops aren't actually related to lamb or sheep? And despite living in Florida near the Everglades for the last several years, I have still never been able to slip the latter into casual conversation. Multiple failed attempts? Oh Yeah.

And did I mention that I was psyched when I made it through the set of World Book Encyclopedias housed on a bookshelf in my room as a kid? Or how about that t-shirt I have always wanted to buy emblazoned with the symbols "$\pi + dx/dy$," which, for those of you who don't read math, says, "Pi plus rate" or "Pirate." Oh, and to wear that t-shirt every March 14th = 3.14 = Pi Day. Like I said, I am a nerd.

And, finally, I never fit in. A shocking discovery I am sure, given self-admission number two and the fact that we moved a lot (more than a military family) when I was a kid. When I was younger, this was problematic. I longed to stay in one place like everybody else and wondered what it must be like to grow up in the same house on the same street with the same people, but, of course, I wasn't like everybody else or so it seemed at the time. Now, it's no big deal and quite frankly I can't imagine being in the same place doing the same thing for more than three to four years. I am actually thankful we moved so often. It gave me a series of do-overs and lots of opportunities to try on different versions of me, knowing that if it wasn't the right fit, we would move again soon and I could try again. In fact, I think it is this constant feeling of displacement that keeps me going now. It fuels my desire to always be exploring and learning.

Alas, I would love to promise you some grand story like *Eat. Pray. Love.*, but no publishing house is willing to give me an advance and put me up for a year of travel for self-exploration. So, although I eat plenty, pray often, and love abundantly, there is no idyllic ending to a totally epic journey around the world. But that would be too predictable, now, wouldn't it?

UNDERSTANDING THE EMOLECULE

I have two strongly held beliefs that are the basis for this book, and for all that I do for that matter. The first is that I don't believe in luck, at least not in the traditional sense of the word. I cannot stand behind the idea that success or failure is merely an act of chance, rather than something that is brought on by one's own actions. The Roman philosopher, Seneca, nailed it on the head (in my opinion) when he supposedly stated, "Luck is what happens when preparation meets opportunity." When we get envious of another's success, it is easy to judge that success on its face and chalk it up to that person's luck. I refuse to do this because of my steadfast belief that nothing is an act of chance, but rather a product of hard work and perseverance. Opportunities don't just magically appear, but rather, they are created and crafted through preparation. In order for me to keep my sanity through the daily grind and give meaning to what I do, I must believe that if I work hard enough, create opportunities, and take action, I will be rewarded with success. I think this might explain why I am such a lousy gambler . . . hmm. And don't get me started on the lottery for those of you who are already calling my belief about luck into doubt. I promise it is not about luck, but rather it is about commercializing statistical probability. But like I said, I'm not going to get started . . .

My second belief is that all people, man, woman, or child,

hold within themselves a little spark, a flame that keeps them going. It is this flame from which dreams are woven. It shines bright and clear for some, but for others it is a faint glow masked behind a cloak or curtain, barely discernible. But this light is part of us whether we recognize it or not. It is our innate characteristic and predisposition as humans to stride forward, seek out opportunity, pursue our dreams or leave a legacy. It is what makes people work hard or start a business, for example. It makes us want to live our destiny and become more or better than what we are today. This inner greatness is what I call the "eMolecule."

Darwin may have referred to his version of it from a purely biological standpoint as survival of the fittest, but we have moved past survival of the fittest in terms of adaptability and food chains, to a point where not only does one have to adapt and survive, but in order to do so, one has to be enterprising, entrepreneurial even. Now, I don't intend to purport that the eMolecule is what has fueled man from cave to castle, but stumbling across fire and applying it to food, in hindsight, is in fact quite enterprising and entrepreneurial, to tag this simple act with the terminology of our day.

It is this so-called eMolecule that lives in each and every one of us. Some of us found it early on in life, for others it took a bit longer, and some still may be unconscious of its very existence. However, it is my belief that anyone has the ability and strength to harness its power in order to find their entrepreneurial spirit if willing to look deep inside. Once found, you will experience a new breed of empowered existence and self-awareness to truly taste what freedom feels like. No matter how lost you may feel, you have what it takes to overcome your fears and find your path to entrepreneurial greatness if you surrender your judgment and give yourself permission to steer your course in a different direction.

My eMolecule wasn't always readily accessible. In fact, finding it has been hard work and even harder still to listen to it and let it guide me. The path to harnessing my eMolecule has been fraught with fear, addiction, love, and discovery. It hasn't been a straight path; it's been messy, yet has given way to blissful moments and a beautiful existence. Now that I am aware and empowered by my eMolecule, I cannot go back and try life without it. I am free. I am liberated. I am finally able to be me, live my life, and pursue my passions. I have granted myself permission to be free from guilt and anxiety. I have stopped trying to force expectations of what my life "should" look like and decided to be okay with what it actually looks like. And since you asked, yeah, life is pretty awesome. The best is yet to come and as long as I let my eMolecule be the compass, my heart will follow. And, that, my friends, is where happiness and fulfillment begins, but it all starts with finding and acknowledging your eMolecule.

This is my journey of discovery and capturing my eMolecule. It is my invitation for you to join me on my journey because although I have traveled a long way already, there is still a very long way to go and lots of work to be done. I ask you to join me because it is a journey not meant to be taken alone and because I need you, just as you need me (and we need each other), as you continue on or embark on your journey. I am not alone. You are not alone. Together we will combine our strengths to overcome our weaknesses. Together we can conquer any obstacle. It can be done alone, but it is much more dangerous. So please, let me share my journey with you. All I ask in return is that you share your journey with me.

With love and gratitude,
MARY TODD

FOREWORD

Despite being confident in who I am and what I have accomplished, my initial reaction in being asked to write the foreword for this book was, "Why me?" I am full of enthusiasm and gratitude about my life and what I have created, and yet that little voice in my brain still said, "Really? You? But why you, of all people? Why not Oprah or Ellen Degeneres or at least someone famous?" That's the voice you must learn not to trust.

While discussing our life paths and career goals over coffee, I asked Mary Todd the question that had been nagging me and suggested that maybe this was a job for a world-changer like Oprah. She said she had considered it briefly until it occurred to her that there was someone in her own backyard that had moved and inspired her deeply, and who exhibits what the eMolecule is all about. "You have enterprised on your passion," she stated.

That statement blew me away. I realized that not only was it true, but that the eMolecule is what the world-changers have in common; a passion so true that it overcomes the voice in our head that asks "Why me?"

Why not you?

My dream was born out of the dissatisfaction of being unable to find a consistent and welcoming yoga class. I know that yoga has the power to heal bodies, minds, and relationships and I was dedicated to creating what I was unable to find for myself, so I did. I went from a one room studio as Bala Vinyasa Yoga to co-owner of six combined Green Monkey studios across South Florida, have taught at Yoga Journal Conferences, and traveled as far as Africa and Israel in my effort to bring yoga to the lives of others. Have I felt fear along the way? Yes, every other freaking day! However, fear and excitement have the same physiological symptoms in the body; it is our perception of the situation that has us in fear. Once I realized that, I learned to embrace my fear as an invitation to growth and began to look forward to whatever the future held, even if it deviated from my original plan. As a result, my business has grown beyond my wildest dreams, and it's just the beginning. Part of living in expression of my eMolecule is to make the extraordinary ordinary in order to motivate myself to reach beyond the current highest standard and when that is your word to yourself, it moves from possibility to probability and then becomes reality.

When your thoughts and actions are in alignment for the greatest intention and you are enthusiastic and open to possibilities, the universe will conspire to make it happen—but not without the personal investment of passion (and a ton of work!) You must authentically share your passion with the world to create big things, as it will speak for your vision more than mere words can. Life is too short not to, for this world needs people who have vitality and who are living into their greatest self by being driven by what they love and loving others.

The greatest gift is when we share our truth, our word, as Mary has done so courageously in *eMolecule*. She connects to the human being on a raw, real level while connecting to her essence of light, love, strength, power and survival. That's what we all desire—to be free, and the *eMolecule* demonstrates that we have the keys to unlock ourselves from our imprisonment of perceptual illusions such as self-doubt and denial; to silence that limitation of "Why me?"

Once you recognize your own power, you are able to act powerfully in any situation, and yet most of us live our lives as if we are victims of circumstance, or of that voice of doubt within, and are blind to our own vast potential. Just as the body has a limitless capacity to break down what it needs at the cellular level for energy, it also does for creation and love. At some point we either choose to own our life as our creation, and love ourselves enough to live powerfully or simply accept what is. *eMolecule* makes it possible to move into your created future by recognizing the possibilities for empowerment, movement, and inspiring change from within.

The same physics that apply to the universe apply to our lives. Much like Newton's Second Law of Motion, as the force acting upon an object is increased, the acceleration of the object is increased, allowing it to continue in a state of motion. We will continue to do what we are doing, think what we are thinking, and say what we are saying until a force of equal impact intervenes; only then will we consider change or a new direction. In other words, change isn't going to be comfortable. Sometimes we actually listen to the soft intervention and shift gears, but many times we need to go through much more and discover for ourselves what is not working in order to make the shift to act in a way which works in our life, relationships, and situations that arise. Whatever the catalyst for change ends up being is not wrong, for how can we know pleasure without pain, light without dark, love without hate, happiness without sorrow, or failure without success? These are all just different experiences that we as human beings go through, none of it has to be wrong—we just need to deal with it.

Life is intended to be full of discovery and wonderment, fun and astonishment. We all have regrets and make mistakes. We all have that doubting voice in our head. We all feel disgust, anger, and judgment of ourselves and others—and with that, your humanity isn't unique or special. Your history doesn't need to define you in a limiting way because yours is the history of so many others. Thoreau said most men die in quiet desperation, because we somehow think we are alone in our separateness.

We may be dealing with different circumstances, but each of us is at battle with the struggles within and we all have to deal with our internal state of being. How we choose to do that identifies who goes on to live powerfully, yet we can only do so when we stop denying our right to be free to act any way in any situation.

When the book states that there are no limits or rules for entrepreneurs, one could take a step back and say, "well, there needs to be rules and limits in business or, really, in life, isn't that how the whole world attempts to organize itself to function together?" Well, in reality, true genius is seeing things others don't and innovation requires the capacity to be unlimited by any perceptual constraints. Being free to dance in the realm of the possibility that we are free to be any way we choose, in any circumstance, is a critical component of the ontological model for being a leader and exercising leadership effectively. So the seemingly audacious statement that there are no rules is correct, there can't be or one will stay stuck, feeling limited within the constraints set forth by the rules. Of course, in business we create guidelines or processes for how to play the game and have a structure in which to excel, yet those guidelines are always up for discussion. You must be willing to throw away any and everything that you have created at any time to make room for growth.

The reality is that life is not happening in the organ we call our brain, and therefore, it is foolish to allow our lives to be limited by our own self-doubt or story that is created in the brain. For most of us, life is constantly an internal state of what we think or feel, or an analysis of what we have or don't have, or what we haven't or should have done. As a result, we miss out on the opportunities that are right in front of us, or more accurately, within us. We are waiting for this or that to end to get to the next thing and our life is just passing us by numbly, or even worse, we are in judgment of life, ourselves, and others, and allow that to hinder our progress.

Despite being multi-dimensional beings, we can occur to others as two dimensional, like a picture or a point in time where someone sees us and then that is their fixed memory of our being, their recollection of who we are. Most of us want to be seen as our most successful self, yet the reality is that we all fear that the skeletons in our closet will expose us as a fraud. Mary so generously shares and exposes hers in this book, not to get attention or sympathy, but simply to demonstrate that you are not alone; that your humanity is not unique. As humans we all have the same things we must deal with: our thoughts, emotions and bodily sensations.

According to ontology, the study of the being, these are the three components of being a human that we just have to deal with even though we don't always deal with it in the expression that is our greatest self. However, we can only discover who we are through who we are not or who we do not want to be, and ultimately, though who we choose to be.

When we choose to come from a contextual framework of love and gratitude for ourselves and others, the world we live in is of love and gratitude. Like Mary, I, too, feel in love with myself through the practice of yoga. It was a vehicle for acceptance, patience and surrender. Love is everywhere you look when you come from a context of love. We usually experience life where we are at, so if we are at self-criticism and self-doubt, that is our experience of the world. Open yourself up to new experiences with the filter of a new perspective and cultivate the confidence and leadership skills to stimulate your eMolecule into action.

Use your past to propel you forward. Allow your fears to empower you with excitement. Connect with others in a genuine way and share your passion and goals with enthusiasm and conviction. Don't expect joy or fulfillment from anyone or anything you do, bring it to everyone and everything you do. This book is a reminder to follow what moves you, inspires you, and motivates you so that you can't wait to get up in the morning even if it kept you up late at night; to create workability with what you already have to work with—your resources, skills, education— and to use what you have as a starting point. Trust that you will learn everything you need to know along the way and that the true richness of life is to share our joy, pain, sorrows, happiness, success and failures with others authentically. We are each other's witnesses to life. As Ram Dass said, "We're all just walking each other home."

And, of course, the most important factor in successful entrepreneurship? To get started!

KIERSTEN MOONEY

PART ONE

PART ONE

I

SWEET GEORGIA BLACK

"If you do not know where you come from, then you don't know where you are, and if you don't know where you are, then you don't know where you're going. And if you don't know where you're going, you're probably going wrong."

TERRY PRACHETT,
I Shall Wear Midnight

Lying on the hood of a black Pontiac Firebird smoking a Camel Turkish Jade cigarette, I looked up at the stars over the southeastern Georgia sky. There was no moon interfering with their twinkle and they shone brightly. They were mocking me, laughing at where I was and where I was headed if I stayed this course.

My heart was fluttering and the inhalation of the menthol cigarette smoke tingled my lungs and jolted my senses. I felt as if I were in a York Peppermint Patty commercial, my pupils constricting and dilating with each inhale and exhale, goose bumps rising on my skin as a nonexistent frigid breeze passed over my body. I knew in that moment I had a decision to make and that whatever decision I made tonight would change and shape my life forever.

I lifted my head and looked around. It was dark, very, very dark. There was a brown cedar-sided house that jutted like a crooked tooth from the skyline of the surrounding pinewoods. It was evident that at one time, it had been someone's treasured cabin or maybe even a cozy weekend retreat. Now, it lay in a forlorn state, longing for someone to come along and see its potential. I could relate to that.

I heard scattered voices in the woods. I could barely make out the faces to the voices. Most of those around me I had never met before. I trusted none of them.

I walked back into the house. I didn't know whose house it was. I think someone had told me it belonged to a guy named Ricky whoever that was. Inside, the house music held everyone captive to its beat while glow sticks cunningly lured anyone looking to escape reality deeper into their swirling tale in the darkness. I tried to resist their spinning siren song, but the music took over and I forgot why I came inside. The beat shifted just enough to awaken me.

Before I could get ensnared again, I shuffled my way to the kitchen in search of a Vick's vapor stick or some chewing gum. There were pine-scented candles lit in the kitchen and more people that I didn't know. The fragrance was thick and heavy in the air, making it difficult to breathe. Maybe it wasn't the candles, maybe it was being trapped with my thoughts or maybe it was the ecstasy.

I finally recognized a face. A girl named Brandi indicated with her hand to come over by her. I didn't argue. As I stood by her side staring at her, she looked so hollow and distorted. I knew I must have looked hollow and distorted too. I hadn't seen daylight in at least six or seven days, let alone eaten anything. My days started and ended at the mercy of a little blue or yellow pill. I personally preferred the ones with dolphins imprinted on them. They reminded me of the beach.

I looked at Brandi again. She smiled and nodded to the heavy rhythm of the beat. Her smile aged her, bringing out the heavy wrinkles around her sagging hazel eyes, prematurely aging her. Her features indicated that she once had been pretty. She had high cheekbones and a petite nose, but her beauty was overshadowed by the darkness she carried. She looked lost, but seemed unaware of it.

I hadn't known Brandi for long. We met four days prior or something like that. Time elapsed, but I couldn't account for its passage. The faces I had been with for the last week or so had picked her up from her trailer. I was introduced to her two young daughters and infant son. I couldn't remember their names, just their innocent faces. I followed the way her son gazed at his mother so adoringly and unapologetically. Her daughters dressed like twins with their hair in braids, just like my mom used to dress my sister and me. I wondered who was watching them now; she didn't have a husband or boyfriend. We'd all spent the last several days together. I wondered if her kids knew where their mommy was or if they missed her. Maybe they were with the Mayor. I faintly recollected that she told me she was the Mayor's daughter.

I panned the room; we were all here: young and old, rich and poor, black and white. We seemed an unlikely collective, but I understood why we'd united. I didn't know these people, but I didn't have to. We were all inexplicably and undeniably connected. We were all afraid of something. Something so unbearable that it paralyzed us in the daylight. Something that was too hard to deal with or too scary, so we joined together in the darkness like ghouls trying to escape our own hauntings. I knew why I was here. I knew what I was afraid of. I also knew that I had to face my fear sooner or later. That's it then. This is over. I made my decision. This was the last time. The night couldn't end fast enough. I never wanted to roll again and I would never go back to Camden County, Georgia. Ever.

I was eighteen years old and it was the first of many times in my life when I would have to stand on the brink and make a course-altering decision. On that night, if I had been privy to how many more times I would be tested on the road ahead, I might have made a different decision.

II

EARLY MORNINGS, LATE NIGHTS

"You're living your days at the moment how a sheep grazes, meandering, not engaged with anything much."

NIKKI GEMMELL,
The Bride Stripped Bare

To the outside world, I had everything going for me. I was enrolled in a prestigious Big Ten university with the lofty designation of a chemical engineering major. On paper, I looked like the overachiever of overachievers. It seemed that my whole life had been training and preparation to get into a good college. I had an impressive list of extracurricular activities and had graduated high school with above a 4.0 grade point average. I had always taken the most advanced classes, scored the highest, and outperformed the competition in academics. People always seemed to think I had big potential and a bright future, effortlessly gliding through life. This scared the shit out of me and couldn't have been further from the truth.

It all began months earlier, when the fear thundered and crashed into my life. I received a form with several columns of check boxes accompanied by a letter from my future university that instructed me to simply check the box next to the major/

career I desired. I panicked. I hadn't really done anything yet. How could I so casually choose my fate? I stared at the box that said "Other" followed by a line where you could purportedly insert your own made-up designation. I seriously considered the "Other" box, but the line following was so short. I couldn't possibly write down everything I wanted to achieve or become on a line less than two inches long.

Naturally, I did what any irrational college entrant would have done: I selected the most impressive and complicated major I could. That way, when people inevitably judged me, they wouldn't ask too many questions about my choice because, after all, who actually knows what chemical engineers do? I certainly didn't know, but it sounds good, right? My strategy worked. Crisis averted. I could continue hiding.

Years later, I would be faced with a similar question in a job interview. The interviewer asked me whether I thought I would be happy doing that particular job forever. I candidly advised her that I could not answer her question with substantial certainty and quite frankly, anyone who affirmatively answered this question was lying. I mean, who professes a lifelong love for sushi before ever setting foot into a sushi bar and trying it for the first time? Needless to say, I didn't get the job. It probably was the right decision on the part of the interviewer; I'm certain I would have hated it, but at least I was honest. That should have counted for something.

Being on campus was surreal. The main quad was a large grassy rectangle with twelve distinct buildings on its perimeter. The quad was anchored on one end by the student union and on the other end by a picturesque auditorium, complete with a copper dome roof. Bronze statues adorned the sidewalks and entrances to several of the buildings. The buildings were old and steeped in history and tradition. To my untrained eye, it looked as if each major architectural period had its place here like some life-sized monument to a bygone era. It felt almost as if at some point in that past, this was the heralded mecca of academia where great thinkers emerged and now it was adulterated with the iPods of pseudo intellectuals and boom boxes of jocks, all here to try to impress someone else or to fit in.

This was the heart of the campus, a meeting place and a cross-roads for travelers to scuttle from building to building. There were girls lounging in the sun on blankets. Nearby a group of guys tossed a football. A group of freshmen stood clutching their books tightly against their chests as they nervously surveyed the crowd. There were people meeting for the first time and people meeting again, getting reacquainted after a summer absence. People from all backgrounds, programs of study, and interests congregated here on this sunny August afternoon. It was warm, but there was a pleasant breeze passing through the trees.

A tour group passed by and fervent future collegiate minds stared in awe at the expansive space. They could taste their imminent freedom that would be taking place in just a few short months. Anxious parents stayed to the back of the group nearly teary eyed, getting glimpses of what it would be like when little Johnny or Becky flew the coop. There was, of course, the parent-child combination at the very front, eagerly peppering the poor tour guide with tons of idiotic questions. No way did I have the patience to put up with that nonsense. I felt bad for the poor student guide. To my right there were two Asian girls trying to a coax a fat squirrel from a tree with almonds. Each time the squirrel flicked his tail they broke out into a fit of giggles. I rolled my eyes. He seemed to enjoy toying with the girls.

I sat under the shade propped up against the base of a tree trunk outside one of the grand halls. School would be starting tomorrow. I wanted to be excited to be here. To share in the frenetic energy that buzzed through the campus. I certainly had something coursing through my veins, but it wasn't excitement.

Although my parents worked hard to afford me the opportunity to go to college, it wasn't quite enough to cover tuition, books, and room and board. We agreed that if I maintained a 4.0 grade point average, they would continue paying an allotted amount of my college expenses and I would be responsible for coming up with the additional monies to bridge the gap. I sensibly got a part-time position working at the college bookstore across from the math building, which had the added benefit of receiving a discount on textbooks and supplies.

When the position at the bookstore proved insufficient to supply enough money to cover my living and recreational expenses, I sought out additional work. I scored a job as the janitor of a laboratory at the Micro and Nanotechnology Laboratory within the College of Engineering. The janitorial position allowed me to keep my own hours, working around my 18 credit hour advanced course load and job at the bookstore. The uninterrupted moments of solace and peace while mopping the floors and cleaning the counters were priceless. The vents that filtered and cycled the air maintaining the particle count in the lab had the effect of a muffling sound, almost like you just walked into a vacuum. It's very similar to how it feels and sounds inside the pressurized cabin of a commercial aircraft. I was safe in here. The madness that ensued beyond the laboratory sanitizing and suit up pre-entrance station, the badge entry into the building wing, and the security checkpoint at the building entrance couldn't reach me in here. Not even my fears or demons could follow me in here. Nothing. My mind left me alone as I methodically mopped the floors. For ten or so hours a week, I could let my guard down and exist. Relax. Breathe.

Outside of the laboratory, my charade was getting more complicated. I sat like a zombie through my classes, going through the motions of homework, research papers, and exams. I barely noticed when the season shifted from the sunny, golden fall to the naked grey of winter. I didn't want to and couldn't face my roommates, look them in the eyes and tell them what was happening. Instead, I hated their prying eyes and concerned looks. I hated that they, too, didn't find themselves in the same place as me. I hated myself. In order to circumvent any chance of contact with them and avoid looking too deeply at myself, I took on another job.

At 4:45 every morning, I took the city bus to the other side of campus to a graduate student dormitory where I helped a disabled masters student get ready for classes. I think he had cerebral palsy. His mobility and speech were severely limited. It was heavy lifting and heartbreaking work, mostly because this shining individual had to depend on me of all people. His day couldn't start without me. He trusted me implicitly for no reason, but he didn't judge me either. He didn't care what I did or didn't do the night before. All I had to do to make him smile was just show up. Unfortunately, there came a day when I just stopped showing up.

I successfully shirked engaging with anyone. I was cast as the lead role in a play that looked good on paper. I helped the graduate student from 4:45 A.M. to 8 A.M., went to back-to-back classes from 8 A.M. until 3 P.M., cleaned the lab until 5 P.M., and worked at the bookstore until closing at 10 P.M. I cannot really account for the time between 10 P.M. and 4:45 A.M. I know I simultaneously dreaded and pined for its arrival. Eventually, whatever happened during these hours took over and I found myself existing only in the darkness. I virtually disappeared from daylight altogether. I was happy that winter was fast approaching. The days were getting noticeably shorter and I could hide in layers of grey wool and knit to pass by pedestrians on the quad undetected, to stay in the darkness.

Sometimes, I would think about my past, trying to connect the dots and figure out how I ended up in this place. I never could get from point A to point B. I had a perfectly idyllic childhood. Seriously, our family could have been the poster family for Country Time Lemonade and Walt Disney World. My older sister and I had everything we needed, but not everything we wanted. We learned to be very practical with our wish lists at birthdays and holidays, because frivolity was not tolerated. If our parents were stressed or hard times fell upon us, we certainly were left blissfully ignorant to that fact.

We learned early on, however, about a hard day's work. As small children, we were never allowed to dodge our household chores and allowances were unheard of. My mom didn't believe we should get rewarded for something we were supposed to do anyway. When we were old enough, we went off to work in the cornfields from dawn until dusk during our summer breaks from school. We worked for Pioneer Seed Company in Adair, Illinois, as corn pollinators. My sister even had a paper route during the school year, delivering newspapers in the rain, snow or shine to the houses in our neighborhood. I was never interested in a paper route. I was much more interested in hawking tie-dyed golf balls and scoring lucrative pet sitting deals. Life was so sweet and so simple.

We were always encouraged to make our own decisions and try new things, forge our own way. We were never pressured to become doctors or lawyers or investment bankers. Our parents promoted and pushed us to choose a path in our lives that would make us happy. As long as we tried our hardest and gave it our all, despite the perfect or imperfect result, that was enough for them. That is all they ever asked of us. Oh yeah, and graduate from college with a "useful" degree.

And yet despite all of this, I still ended up in the Middle of Nowhere, Georgia, on the bender of all benders, wasting myself away with people I didn't even know. No one knew where I was. I could have easily slipped away into the darkness forever. It was tempting, too tempting. But it was my mother who saved me in that moment, standing in the kitchen of that brown house. In hindsight, she's the one who always ended up saving me in the difficult times that I had yet to face.

She sacrificed so much in her life: a college education, pursuing her life's dream to be an art teacher, and who knows what else, to dedicate herself to giving her daughters every opportunity a mother could. I could live with disappointing myself, but I could not let her sacrifices be made in vain. I could not bring myself to destroy her.

III

BEING NORMAL IN NORMAL

"When we played our charade we were like children posing;
playing at games, acting out names, guessing the parts we played."

HENRY MANCINI,
lyrics from Charade

I wish I could say that I did a complete 180-degree flip and all was rainbows and roses, but quite obviously that isn't the case, as you can clearly tell, because there are more pages in this book . . . and sorry to ruin the surprise, but they're not blank either.

Believe it or not, I actually finished that first semester in college with all 'A's. However, I didn't hold up my end of the bargain; an A- in my five-credit Calculus 2 and Calculus 3 combined level class was the demise of my 4.0 grade point average. Maybe my parents would have paid for another semester, but it wouldn't have mattered. I would have dropped out anyway. I needed to live life, but I was choosing to live all the wrong moments.

I moved back home and enrolled in the local community college. I honestly can't remember if I paid for it or if my parents footed the bill. My guess is that they were gracious enough to cover the costs. I can only really recall a few things from those months: my nights were now spent in a memory-less, alcohol-and-drug-drenched daze; I had straight As in all my classes, but got kicked out of school anyway because I never showed up to class except on exam days. I engaged in my usual routine of over-committing myself, so I wouldn't have to deal with anything. I needed to stay busy, and I needed money. I was somehow clean enough to pass a blood screening, so I sold my blood plasma two times per week for $127, worked as a salesclerk and seamstress at a bridal and formalwear shop, as a lifeguard, and as the take-out girl at a local Chinese restaurant; and I got reacquainted with my high school flame.

He was the best thing and the worst thing that could have happened to me. He was tall and thin, but strong. His features overwhelmingly disclosed his Polish heritage. He had a gentle crooked smile that softened his hardened steel-blue eyes and straw-colored hair. He was mysterious, in an angst-y musician sort of way, an anguished soul, while I was just ordinary. I was drawn to him like a moth to a flame. I always had been, even in high school. We went to prom together and we loved each other as much as any kids could. Our relationship ended involuntarily when my family moved to a new town again and long distance relationships just didn't work for teenagers at that time. I mean, we couldn't Skype, and there were no cell phones. Heck! I had just gotten my driver's license!

When we met again as adults, it was as if nothing had changed between us. We had a connection, and we believed that it was fate or destiny that had brought us together again or something like that. The truth was, we were both broken. We were both addicts and we needed each other's support to lessen the loneliness and justify our decisions. For some reason, my choices seemed okay if he approved them and vice versa. It was easier not having to look inside myself for the right answers. I could place that burden on someone else who wouldn't search as deeply.

I also needed him because I had nowhere to go anymore. All bridges leading back home were burned, and I couldn't blame anyone but myself. Now, looking back, I am certain that at least one bridge was always available. I envision the bridge back home like one of those rope bridges you imagine in the Amazon or someplace wild that is barely hanging on by a thread of rope across a deep ravine with raging waters nearly indiscernible in the distance below except for the thunderous echo in the canyon. The bridge could have been there, and probably was, but I was too afraid to look and certainly too ashamed to attempt crossing it.

He needed me because he yearned to be loved; his heart needed to mend. Downtrodden from a very rough upbringing with little means to escape his past, he, like his older siblings, turned to music, drugs, and alcohol. In that regard, they are all musical prodigies and some of the smartest people I have ever met. In fact, it is still hard for me to swallow that fact that three extraordinarily brilliant and gifted individuals came out of that old dilapidated white Victorian house near the center of town.

Like Brandi, they all seemed oblivious to the fact that they were lost. Maybe they weren't, maybe they just had to flee their past and the only way they knew how was to go out on their own. His older brother fled to Los Angeles and set up a recording studio. He recorded several albums for unknown artists, but he was happy doing his own thing, not relying on anyone else except himself. His older sister left right after college and headed to Berkeley. She was a piano prodigy and continued piano pedagogy studies out west. She set up a piano studio in her backyard and gave lessons, charging whatever the students' families could pay. Sometimes she received food, other times it was money. The payment didn't matter. She lived for the teaching.

It truly was him and his family that showed me there was more out there in the world than mere check boxes on a form; that there was something internal that drove them to do what they did. Yes, they were escaping their pasts, but they were shaping their futures and making their own rules. They had the power to decide. That is when I recognized they had looked inside and found something very special: an *eMolecule*.

When the two of us were in California visiting his brother and sister I had a chance to meet their friends, a group of artists, musicians, and innovators that were all paving their own way. They defied the boundaries of the traditional nine-to-five that I had been raised to think was the prize.

They all have eMolecules. How? How do they do it? No one seems to "go to work" and when they work, they are doing what they love. This makes no sense to me. Life is about being practical and doing what is expected.

I looked around the room sizing up each individual. They didn't get there by accident. They chose to be there. Just like they chose to set out their own shingle doing something they loved, following their passions. That's when I realized there was an *eMolecule* that existed inside each and every one of us. Out of necessity or free will, it was there to help you, no matter what. But there's a catch: *only you can make the choice to embrace your eMolecule.*

I want to find my eMolecule, too. That choice proved harder than I ever thought.

He and I were living in a warped Jackson Pollock story intermixed with twisted delusions from *A Beautiful Mind.* There was pain and incoherent brilliance. I saw so much potential in him. He had such raw talent. He was so much smarter than I could ever dream of being, but he failed to see it. He had such natural talent, not only for music, but for hard sciences and math and yet I sat idly by watching him waste it, growing more frustrated at our circumstances.

In the beginning, we professed drug-and alcohol-induced statements of grandeur, wild spontaneity, and passion. When the fire burned, it was white hot. When it wasn't lit, it was ice cold. He was abrasive, to put it mildly. Despite his efforts to forget, he was like his father. He had a raging temper with an aggressive mean streak. I would cower in a corner and whimper. Then, his temperament would unexpectedly flip and he would come begging apologetically for forgiveness. We played tormented lovers well; it fit the ups and downs of getting high.

He was very controlling and jealous. He kept meticulous tabs on me for no reason. He said he trusted me but acted to the contrary. He always claimed that it was other guys that he didn't trust and in my naiveté, I believed him. I assumed he was just trying to protect me. I stopped wearing makeup to avoid the relentless rounds of questioning and taunting before I left the house. "I thought you were just going to class. Who are you trying to impress?" I would catch him stalking me around campus, lurking in the shadows, checking up on me to make sure I was indeed going where I said I was going. If I stopped to talk or made eye contact with anyone I passed, I would get grilled later, so I just kept my gaze toward my feet and avoided interactions.

He knew what he was doing. He would tell me that I was his world, his everything, and he would be dead inside without me. His life would no longer be worth living if I ever left. In the beginning, this seemed like epic love, but it really was just a means to keep me in cage. The less I ventured into the outside world, the greater control he could exercise over me. I would continue to be broken, while he grew stronger from my weakening. It was oppressive and suffocating, but I had neither the self-confidence nor the courage to stand up for myself or leave, even when it worsened. And he knew it. Being brave is hard and I was not up to the challenge.

Still rejecting the idea that I could do something undefined, or rather undiscovered, at least to me, I forged on blindly. I did the only things I knew how to do: work, take classes, and stay numb through whatever means necessary. I continued to enroll in classes, this time at Illinois State University. I only disclose that because it is located in Normal, Illinois, and I find this rather ironic. And no, I never lived on Normal Street in Normal. I certainly would have gotten evicted.

IV

WEDDING MOURNING

"There are things of which I may not speak; There are dreams that cannot die; There are thoughts that make the strong heart weak, and bring a pallor into the cheek, and a mist before the eye."

HENRY WADSWORTH LONGFELLOW

It was the day of my wedding. It was raining. *Is it good luck or bad luck to rain on your wedding day?* I wondered. *Well, it seems appropriate for me.*

I sat in a gilded King Louis XVI-style chair with pink velvet upholstery in front of an English country scene frescoed on the wall behind me, staring out at the raindrops pelting the window-panes. On the sidewalks below, pedestrians and city dwellers dashed and darted about for cover from the unexpected summer rain shower.

My wedding gown draped gracefully around the legs of the chair, my light blue sash emphasized the twirl in the fabric like a funnel. To an onlooker, I looked as if I could have been in a still-life oil painting from another era: my stoic eyes with their piercing stare and the corners of my mouth curving slightly downward to create an imperceptible frown. I must have looked lovely, like a princess of a bygone age. I was even wearing a tiara.

But I was mourning. My stomach was in knots and I could barely swallow. I was aflutter. No, butterflies would have been too gentle; I was swarming with bees and wasps inside. The swirl of my sash and train felt like a whirlpool sucking me down into the depths of Lake Michigan, gasping for air. I was clawing and scratching, but there was nothing to grasp, my motions just pushed through the water creating tiny bursts of bubbles, but I was still sinking down. It took all of my willpower and strength to maintain my composure.

I closed my eyes and envisioned that bridge in the jungle. *Is it still there? Is it possible to find it? Have I strayed too far to turn back now?* I wanted nothing more than to scream at the top of my lungs, *call the whole thing off,* but I couldn't. To call it off would mean that I would have to admit things to my family, but more importantly, to myself. I would have to crawl out from behind my shield. He had been my deflector, my scapegoat. If I no longer had him, what did I have? I didn't even know who I was. I wasn't sure if I was strong enough to stand alone. I couldn't face myself. So, I did the most horrible thing a person could do to another person: *I lied.*

I walked down that aisle knowing that I was marrying a man that I didn't deserve, and yet, he didn't deserve me either. I knew when I said, "I do" that I was lying. Not just to a man that I was supposed to unconditionally love, but to my family, to my friends, and to God. There wasn't a question of love. I loved him the only way I knew how, but not in the same sense that I understand love today. I depended on him and needed him like a drug addict needs the next score.

No one asked me to dance at my wedding reception. I largely sat alone in the corner of the yacht trying to swallow what I had just done. I watched the sun melt into the horizon casting its fiery warning across the water and the sky. The glittering Chicago skyline bustled with energy and life as we floated along the lakeshore into darkness. It was breathtaking and ominous.

For anyone who has walked into a marriage knowing and

feeling what I felt, my heart goes out to you. For anyone who has been brave enough to call it off, I salute you for your courage. I know what it must have taken, but I myself was too weak to muster that gumption. You are braver than me.

After the reception, when we walked into the lobby at the Hilton Hotel on Michigan Avenue, everyone stopped to applaud and congratulate our nuptials. I felt as if they all stopped in their tracks because they could smell a weasel. They could tell I had just perpetrated fraud on mankind. I wanted to vomit.

I went up to our suite. I called the concierge to have a robe and cheeseburger with a Sprite delivered. I hadn't eaten anything all day. My newly minted husband never showed up to the suite that night. He spent the night drinking scotch with his friends and family, reveling in the day's events and gloating in his marital success. I changed out of my dress and solemnly choked down a few bites of cheeseburger. I called my mom that night to confess what I had done.

"Mom, I just married a man knowing that we are going to get divorced. I'm all alone right now. I don't think he will even be with me tonight. This isn't the way it's supposed to happen." I sniveled between stifled sobs and whimpers.

I heard my mom stifling sobs and tears of her own. "My heart goes out to you, Mary. It really does. I wish there was something I could do to protect my little girl from this hurt. It hurts me so much knowing you hurt like this."

"I don't know what to do."

"All you can do for right now is try to get some sleep. It has been a long emotional day for everyone. I love you. I love you so much. I love you more than I can tell you."

"I love you too, Mom."

I cried myself to sleep that night.

I can't imagine my mom slept at all that night or most nights for that matter.

That night was indicative of most of the nights in my marriage: spent alone crying.

I know in my heart that I didn't have to make that phone call; that I didn't have to tell my mom anything. She knew. She had always known. She knew when I disappeared to Georgia. She knew all of my lies and yet somehow she had the strength to trust me and the faith that I would prevail knowing that interfering would only have driven me deeper. I admire that about her.

Mom, I love you.

V

STUPID SILVER TRAY

"You often meet your fate on the road you take to avoid it."

GOLDIE HAWN

One of the benefits of living in my lie was that I learned how to cook. In my attempt to play Happy Housewife, I made it a point to be overly domesticated. It was my cry out to the world that I was trying to be different from my old self. I was trying to move onto a different path, but still protect myself from others. I still didn't want people to *see me* for who I really was. I was ashamed and fearful. So I created another shell around me to protect me from their criticism.

Oh, I tried to be so completely opposite of what I had been. It's like I went in as me and came out as Patty Duke on the other side, minus the housedress and heels accompanied by perfectly manicured nails and an artfully applied face. By the same token, I knew I wasn't happy, but I wasn't brave enough to fix it either. On the other hand, I was a lot happier than I had been, so maybe this was as good as it was supposed to get for me. Regardless, it gave me something to focus my energy on. It gave me another layer of safety. I was trying to be like a magician: diverting the audience's attention away while I slyly slipped the rabbit out of the hat unnoticed. I thought that if I put on this charade, then no one would really look at me, including myself.

I redecorated the shabby little house we lived in. This is when I met IKEA for the first time, and it has been a long and happy union so far. I wait with baited breath for the new IKEA catalog each year. Oh, those glossy pages full of such carefully thought out and practical Scandinavian furniture! How you bring such smooth lines and efficiency to my life! I already told you I was an addict, so I had to replace my vices . . . my current house could probably double as an IKEA showroom.

In my zealous attempt at housewife perfectionism, I expanded my domesticated repertoire from cross-stitching and crocheting, to embroidery and macramé. I pretty much took up all things related to housekeeping and signed up for a subscription to the domesticated womens' bible: *Martha Stewart Living*. If you ever want to learn anything related to housewifery, Martha is your gal, and she can do everything you can do, but better, like folding fitted sheets. Mine still don't come out folded the same size as the flat sheet, but oh well. (At least I can say that now.)

Everyone who attended will no doubt remember the over-the-top Thanksgiving feast I prepared complete with palate cleansers between courses, even if the pomegranate-cardamom granitas were a total bust. I had even arranged fresh sage leaves in a star pattern underneath the turkey skin. Yes, I do believe that Martha Stewart herself would have been proud. Did I mention that I sewed the tablecloths, table runners, dinner napkins, and cocktail napkins, too? I even painted glitter on squash—yes, everything needed to be dressed up for the holiday.

I became even more engrossed in the perfectness of the lives depicted in the magazine. The feasts that were prepared for casual backyard get-togethers were like nothing I had experienced as a child and everything I wanted my life to be like now. I wanted this marriage to be a relationship full of laughter in a blueberry patch, whilst we and our nonexistent but equally perfect friends all sit on a blue plaid blanket with color coordinated clothing under the dappled sunlight of a maple tree, savoring succulent little pearls of indigo glory and sipping rosemary lemonade spritzers—instead of the abusive addicted hell that was now my reality.

Oh, and the feasts on those pages! Madras plaid clad men carrying platters of grilled-to-perfection lemon-thyme chicken to the impeccably set table in a charming barn adorned with heaping bowls of watercress vichyssoise, bright, juicy melon slices wrapped with paper-thin prosciutto, and a salad of leeks, baby artichokes and goat cheese. My childhood dinners typically involved breaded chicken or pork chops, a Lipton noodle or rice side, and a reheated frozen or canned vegetable. I knew how to prepare food from my childhood. Tuna casserole or stuffed peppers? No problem! But I had no idea that this whole other world of food existed, and I lacked the experience to prepare it. Everything was so new to me. I treasured those magazine pages as if they were printed with gold, reading and then re-reading the issue at least a dozen times. It was a fairytale every month spinning intricate tales of fantasies to daydream and wish for . . . someday. Someday, domesticated glory would be mine!

I made a scrapbook of seasonal decorating ideas or home projects I wanted to try and another just for the recipes. I collected recipes like a kid collects baseball cards. They were my net worth at the time. I still have that binder. It's dark blue with nothing on the spine or front to indicate its importance. I doubt it will ever make it into the digital age and that's okay. It wouldn't be the same anyway. I can flip through those yellowed pages now, the recipes starting to come unstuck as the glue ages and gives up, and remember where I was when I placed that recipe there or when I made it for the first time. More importantly though, it reminds me where I used to be. It makes me feel peaceful to know that I was there and I find solace in those days, but am happy that I never have to go back.

Like most people afflicted with addiction, I dove in head first, no questions asked, into the world of food. I had an insatiable palate for learning about new food cultures and cuisines, about flavors that only existed in my wildest dreams. Every Wednesday I made chocolate chip cookies. I began to replace shot-soaked Saturday nights with all-night cooking festivals. Weekend benders turned into weekend-long baguette baking marathons. My refrigerator and freezer were always chock full of home-cooked meals just needing a quick warm up. It was therapy that was always there for me. All I had to do was turn on the oven or preheat a pan. The kitchen became my sacred safe haven where I could quiet my mind and just create food.

Cooking consumed my spare time. Yes, I had pleasure in tasting the food, allowing it to transport me away from that tiny sage-green kitchen to a far off land, but it was the preparation that I loved: the process of coaxing new flavors out of ordinary ingredients or how the tiny addition of a single spice could change the flavor profile of an entire dish. *I had control over the outcome.* I was given the framework for success, the recipe, but I had the power to change it, adapt it, play with it, and make it *my way.* I poured my heart and soul into every recipe I tried and every dish I made. Over time, it became a vehicle for communicating my love.

There are many sayings about the power of food. I can attest to that power. Through the simple act of preparing food, I began to realize that outcomes are a result of my actions. I began to recognize that everything is a choice. Yes, I knew that every act I took had consequences, but that never really hit home. I knew my actions up to this point had consequences, but I ignored them and forced myself into pretending all was well. *I chose to be exactly where I was and where I am now.* However, when cooking, if a recipe didn't turn out well, I had no one to blame but myself. Conversely, if something turned out divine, I did it! It was me! *All me!* Cooking held me accountable. It forced me to be honest with myself, at least in the kitchen. I didn't know it at the time, but the simple act of cooking was helping my eMolecule shine even brighter. Heck, it was making me shine brighter.

One day at a time, one recipe at a time, I began to look at *my* outcome. Where I'd ended up so far. I started to look at me from an outside perspective. I started to examine myself the same way I tasted a recipe to test the seasoning. I became my own cooking experiment. I had been given the framework of success, just like a recipe. My mother and father had instilled this in me since childhood, but it was me who controlled the result. Everything was a mess simply because I was not heeding the instructions and was using the wrong ingredients. I was haphazardly mixing together ingredients and hoping for cake, but getting a shit sandwich instead. Yet I ended up blaming the ingredients for not giving me the desired the result, but not once blaming myself for using the wrong ingredients. My life was going to turn out like an over-whipped soufflé: neither of us would have the potential to rise, if I didn't start preparing my life with the same attention and methodology as my cooking. *But I had to choose.*

I realized all of this while sitting in our overstuffed olive-green club chair by the obviously fake fireplace in our living room. My cat, Chester, was sitting on the mantle knocking twenty-five-cent IKEA tea light candle holders onto the brick hearth, delighting in their shatter, while I was re-reading an article about Thai curries. The curries seemed so exotic. Silky coconut laced with lemongrass and ginger, spiked with piquant pepper pastes. I closed my eyes expecting to take in the smell of sweet spice. I was surprised when instead I got the taste of hot, salty tears. The walls I had so meticulously built to protect myself from the world started to crack.

It was late, and I was alone. He was due home hours ago, but as usual he didn't call. He was out with the guys playing poker, drinking, and getting high or maybe he was with the guys in his band pulling an all-night recording session, drinking, and getting high. I was trying to clean up my act and his extracurriculars were no longer my desired extracurriculars. I wanted the drugs out of my house. I was furious when I found a huge stash hidden in our basement that he was selling.

"How could you be so stupid?!?" I screamed at him late one night.

"What? We need money," he retorted.

"Well, we wouldn't need money if you hadn't gambled away $5,000 LAST WEEK playing POKER! What the fuck is wrong with you?!? You have a family now! Chester and I need you! You have responsibility now! We have bills to pay! Get your act together and start acting like an adult! I'm trying but it's impossible around here. This place is disgusting! Your friends are disgusting! You are disgusting!"

I laid into him hard. We were swiping at each other's throats. I stomped off to the bedroom, slamming and locking the door behind me. I heard him flee out the door furiously and take off in our car. He didn't come home for three days.

As I sat in the chair, I felt so small and lonely. I wanted to be loved, just plain loved, none of this bullshit with strings attached. No drugs. No alcohol. Just stone sober love. *If what we have is love, I'd rather be alone. I shouldn't hurt all of the time.* I wanted to him to be my husband, to come home to me and act like he gave a shit. Now that we were married, he seemed to have a false sense of security about our relationship. Like he had captured his prize so the hard part was over. He had his wife now, so it was carte blanche permission to do whatever he pleased whenever he pleased. He wasn't being fair to me. He wasn't giving me a chance to try and succeed. The more I talked about my future, about trying to find my calling, the more oppressive he became when he would get home.

A knot worked its way into my throat. I tried to swallow, but couldn't as I realized we were heading in two different directions or at least traveling at two different speeds. I lay in bed alone, like most nights, but knew I had reached the end of my line. I couldn't keep up the charade unless things started to change because I was definitely making the choice to change.

The next morning, I put my heart and soul on a plate, accompanied with a wedge of black forest ham, leek, and Gruyere frittata. It was my last offering of love, the final boarding call. I carried it into the bedroom on a silver tray with a cup of freshly squeezed grapefruit juice, a mug of steaming hot coffee, and a bowl of sliced strawberries. I tried to rouse him to surprise him with a breakfast beaming of my love. When he rejected the offering, he rejected me.

It was unfair, I know, to put that much pressure on the preparation and outcome of one meal, but what can I say? It wasn't the first time he had chosen gambling, guitars, drugs, or alcohol over me. And, I didn't know how much of a profound impact that one decision that morning would have on me. But that morning, as I stood in the bedroom, holding that stupid silver tray, completely dejected and numb from head to toe, I felt a little bit more alive, even just the slightest bit lighter.

VI

FAREWELL, CHICAGO

"The only person you are destined to become
is the person you decide to be."

RALPH WALDO EMERSON

Guess what? Marriage doesn't change anything, except for last names. Well, maybe that's not correct either, because it changed me or at least I changed while I was married. I started to learn that I matter.

It was the beginning of November. I was sitting in the closet in our bedroom staring at the suitcase I had packed.

We had recently moved to the South Side of Chicago against my will. We lived in a dingy apartment on the wrong side of the tracks. Turns out, we landed smack dab in the middle of two rivaling South Side gangs. The sound of sirens in the middle of the night kept me awake, while the sound of gunshots froze my trembles. Most nights, he wasn't home with me. He was out with his cousin or on a call. He had uprooted us from Normal, where I was just starting to get things right, to this dump, all in pursuit of becoming a volunteer firefighter. That's right, *volunteer,* aka not paid. I felt like it was an intentional plot against me, against my progress of self-discovery and recovery.

If this sounds resentful, it's because I resented him at the time. We couldn't afford our rent and bills. We only had one car that usually didn't start, and if it did start, he took it or "needed" it so that he could respond to fire calls, which meant I was on foot or bicycle. I had enrolled in yet again another college, trying to at least stay in school. It took me nearly an hour to get to class in the morning. I took classes until noon and then headed to my job in the liquor department at Walgreens, where I worked until closing five nights a week. It wasn't in the nice part of town. We kept pepper spray under the counter. Yeah, right! Just the sort of thing I want to do when being held at gunpoint; I think I'll just pass out all the cash in the register. Thank you very much. Good thing I never had to test that scenario out.

When working full time at Walgreens proved to be insufficient to cover our bills, I got a job as a bartender at a local bar down the street from our apartment building. I started working there on weeknights, after my shift ended at Walgreens. The bar was an old house that had been converted. The bar area stood in what was presumably the living room at the front of the house; there was a pool table in the dining room. It seemed that only the bathroom and kitchen remained the same, exactly the same. Certainly not up to building code and definitely not up to health code. There was only one bathroom complete with an avocado green bathtub and stained shower curtain clinging onto the curtain rod with just a few broken rings. I'm guessing that the shower at the Bates Motel was cleaner than this one. I never went in that bathroom and most definitely never cleaned it; I was afraid to take out the garbage and get poked by a used syringe. I'm also guessing no one even took notice of my poor housekeeping.

All of the booze was locked in the hallway closet between the kitchen and the bathroom. All of the cash was kept in a tan and green tackle box behind the bar. It looked just like the Plano tackle box I had when I was a kid, except rolls of coins stood in the slots for lures and stacks of bills filled the large bottom compartment where I would have kept the reel and compartmentalized discs of hooks and weights. There was a broken cash register with a pad of paper on top for "ringing up" tabs. Next to that was a jar wrapped in paper scrawled with "Tiping [sic] Ain't in China."

The bar's clientele was an eclectic mix of unemployed, subsidized, or "self-employed" men and women. There were the regulars, who came every night to spend whatever they had been able to gather during the day on 24-ounce Pilsner-Urquell drafts—always just $2. There was the occasional homeless person who would come in just to get warm. They typically would just ask for a book of matches and then leave again. There were the drug dealers. They stood out, always with a ringleader and a supporting posse, strutting around like they were invincible. Those deals usually went down in the dining room by the pool table, and depending on what was exchanged, finished up in the bathroom. Afterwards, it was either shots of Petron or Hypnotic and Hennessey for the crew. The dealers usually left big tips. Well, they were the only ones that really left tips. I was grateful because I needed the money, but scared as hell.

I clearly did not belong there, but I pretended to be tough. I'm sure any one of those guys in there could see my bluff. I guess it didn't matter because they could also tell I would never say a word about what I saw to anyone.

I closed down the bar every weeknight around two in the morning. I worked there alone, and always dreaded this part of the night. The streets were desolate, but I could always hear yells in the distance. I would try not to let my imagination get the best of me as I locked up the doors and walked back to the apartment alone. My earnings were stuffed into my pockets, sometimes I even carried them in a brown paper lunch bag hoping that if I got confronted on my way home, it would be easier just to hand of all the money in a bag instead of having to empty my pockets. Maybe they would just take the money and leave me alone since I was so accommodating.

I always wore a hooded sweatshirt and kept my head facing down. I tried to look as inconspicuous as possible, but felt like a circus sideshow as I walked home. I could feel eyes in the darkness watching me approach, glued to my back as I silently passed by. My heart would be racing, adrenaline pumping through my body in full on fight-or-flight mode, just in case. Now, I know I don't believe in luck, but back then on those walks home, I was truly lucky. Nothing ever happened. I didn't speak and no one spoke to me.

So yes, I resented him for the entire situation. For not making a financial contribution to our partnership; for making me endure that walk five times per week; for being selfish in his career desires; for not taking me and my needs or desires into account. Mostly, I resented him for making me be alone so much, when all I really wanted was to feel loved and needed, to feel important even if just in a small way, or to feel that he would worry about me if I didn't come home one night. But instead, I usually came home to an empty apartment. I felt like an outcast in my own home and in my own marriage. I didn't want this. I didn't ask for this, but then again, I didn't speak up against it either.

In an effort to close the gap on the amount of rent that went onto my VISA card every month, I bought bolts of vintage fabric on eBay and at the Swap-A-Rama to sew into dresses. And yes, money was tight, so I stole deodorant sticks from Walgreens to swap for money to buy fabric a few times. Turns out deodorant sticks are a pretty hot commodity at a swap meet. We didn't qualify for government assistance because I was a student. Although I'm not proud, I guess I did what I had to do to make it work. I suppose I could have always chosen worse things.

I set up a website where I posted images of fabric swatches along with four of the dress styles I could make fairly easily. Purchasers selected their desired fabric and dress style, entered in their measurements, and voila!—three weeks later, they would have a custom made vintage-style dress guaranteed to fit or their money back. I sold those dresses for $180 apiece. The money was a godsend, but my schedule was unbearable. I didn't make it through that semester's classes.

At the time, I didn't know anything about operating a business. I just knew that it needed to work. In fact, when I got started, I didn't even think of it as a business. It merely was a means to an end—the only way I could think of to make money. I was me using whatever talent or skill I had to put food on the table. I have come to realize that was actually me, letting my eMolecule take over. It was like a fight-or-flight response; I had no control over my actions, but rather it was human nature taking over and using some deep-down innate survival instinct when my survival was in question. This instinct lies within all of us and we're all capable of using it.

If you're fortunate, you have a choice, whether or not you choose to use it. You know who you are. You sit at your desk in your cubicle or office and daydream about what it would be like if you took charge of your life, calling the shots for yourself. You find yourselves talking yourself out of taking the plunge: the practicality, the risk, the possible financial strain. You are held back by fear and self-doubt. You, my friends, are the fortunate ones, the ones that have the luxury to ponder and think about action. You have the luxury to choose to act, but you don't have to. Things are comfortable enough for you keep the status quo. And that's fine, but then I don't ever want to hear you complaining about the choice you made or didn't make. And I say all that as a hypocrite because I, too, would find myself later faced with this luxury of decision and complain about it.

But for now, I was having a stare down with that suitcase. I heard the deadbolt unlatch and then heard him coming through the front door. I held my breath. I didn't want him to find me, but I knew he would. He came into the bedroom and his gaze immediately went to my tear-streaked face and finally rested on the suitcase. I closed my eyes and prayed, *"Dear God, I know we don't really talk very much. I am afraid. I want this to be over. I have made mistakes, but I'm willing to do what it takes to overcome them. Please, please give me the strength to stand my ground, if only for five minutes. I'll just take five minutes pleeeeaaaasssse. Something. . .anything. . ."*

His wail shattered my prayer. It was like nothing I had ever heard before and I hope never to hear again. It was raw, guttural, almost inhuman bellowing from the inner depths of man. All emotions, anger, joy, hatred, sorrow, guilt, happiness, that had ever been contained or suppressed in his life came exploding out at once like water that had been forcefully pent up behind a dam for decades, then all of a sudden cracks into a million tiny fragments in an instant. The sound wrenched at every emotional string in my being. I could hear the heartbreak and feel my heartache. I could hear the honesty. I could hear the realization and self-admission that this had never been right. We'd been living a lie, and for the first time he recognized or admitted it, too. And then flowed the tears.

A suitcase had just turned our lives upside down. A suitcase had just given me an audience. A suitcase finally made me heard . . . *a suitcase.* And even more miraculously, when I went to speak, I had the strength to do so. I stopped lying and started telling the long overdue truth. It hurt. It stung. Sometimes, I even felt it lash across my face, but it didn't matter. I created the pain myself and would have to face it sooner or later, and *I chose sooner. I chose now.*

After four years of co-dependency, our journey together ended. I was finally brave enough to stand on my own two feet, to stand alone. I was ready to find out who I would become and define me by my own standards.

VII

CHESTER

"If having a soul means being able to feel love and loyalty and gratitude, then animals are better off than a lot of humans."

JAMES HERRIOT

One summer before he and I married, a small three-and-a-half-pound nude tabby meandered into my life. He had inquisitive blue eyes and a leopard print collar with a purple heart-shaped tag emblazoned with the name Dr. Hannibal Lector. His owners had recently found him, brought him in, and decided they were unable to keep him. They intended to put this sweet, tiny creature back outside where they found him, so I leapt to the rescue.

I knew virtually nothing about cats and cat care, except that he was really cute and his current name had to go. I renamed him Mr. Chester Whiskers. Very respectable, don't you think? Chester became my best friend and ultimate companion. I desperately needed someone to confide in and he desperately just wanted to have his chin scratched. We were perfect for each other.

They say that animals have a sixth sense; that they can tell your emotions or know if something is wrong before you do. There is no shortage of amazing stories about pets saving their owners. They are truly selfless servants. All they ask for is a fresh bowl of water, some food, and love, lots and lots of love. Then, they are yours forever. Always by your side and always there for you. There seems to be some widespread misconception that cats, in particular, are loners, that they are independent creatures and they prefer to hide when new people are introduced into their environment. This has not been my experience, but rather the complete opposite has been true.

Chester came to me during a pivotal time when I knew that my husband and I were moving apart, but I wasn't brave enough to face to the truth yet. I was lonely. I cried a lot. I was awake at night worrying about money or being angry with him for gambling away six months of rent money. Chester became my partner when I felt that my own partner had abandoned me. He would sit so patiently, like a mother cradling her young, with my face plunged into his soft, furry belly as I let out bellows and bales from a breaking heart, disappointment, shame, and withdrawal. He looked back at me with such love and care as I cried out rhetorically, *"WHY?!? WHY, God, are you letting this happen to me? I know I have burned through all of my chances, but just please give me one more. This time I won't mess up. I promise. This time will be different. I am putting those days behind me. I will not purposefully hurt myself anymore."*

In raging anger and hatred, when all I wanted to do was lash out on the world and on the people I loved, Chester would fearlessly rub up against my leg and let out a gentle meow, reminding me that anger will not solve any problem. His subtle reminder would instantly soften my brow and by the time I reached down to give him a "Thank you for reminding me not to kill anything" chin scratch, my anger would subside and give way to guilt.

Chester and I were inseparable. At home, he was either on my lap or sitting propped up on my hip like a toddler. I took him to classes with me. I couldn't find anything in the university handbook that stated to the contrary, so I figured I would keep bringing him until someone told me otherwise. Nobody every confronted me, but Chester and I got many shocked double takes as people spun around to confirm that they really had just seen a cat walking down the hallways on a leash. Chester loved the attention. He is a regular ol' ham. He revels and basks in the glory of being the center of attention, and man, does he ham it up. He "plays cute" really, really well and he knows it, too, which makes it impossible to get angry with him when he does something he's not supposed to do.

Just as you think you are going to hang him out of the window on the end of a flagpole by his collar, right after your face becomes bright red like a cartoon but right before steam starts to blow out of your ears, he flips over onto his back, baring his fluffy white belly, cocks his head and gives you the most wide-eyed, innocent stare that just says, "Wwwhhhhaaaat? Mmmmeeeeee? I could never be naughty. Look at this face and then tell me you don't love me." The worst part is, it works like a charm every time.

This works out really well for Chester because he lives up to every stereotype about cats and their endless curiosity. Just like me, he is an envelope-pusher in every aspect of the term. His favorite game (still) is to push glass objects onto tile flooring and watch them shatter. I cannot count the number of glasses, candleholders, and alarm clocks that saw their demise at the paws of Chester.

He also is never deterred by the typical cat deterrents. Take, for example, the use of aluminum foil and tape, which is commonly used to aid cat owners trying to teach their cats not to jump on a particular surface. According to this wisdom, placing aluminum foil sheets on the surface, coupled with tape sticky side up, prevents cats from hanging out on the surface. Conventional wisdom states that cats don't like the sound of aluminum foil when they walk across it and that they most certainly dislike the feeling of tape sticking to their paws. Um, nice try folks, but I think not. Chester loves the sound of aluminum foil and the fact that it is shiny. It's like crack to him. And the sticky side of tape—He. Loves. It. If given the opportunity, he will lick all of the sticky glue off of any type of tape. In fact, he comes running every time he hears the telltale sound of a roll of packing tape in use. Clearly, this tactic had the effect of making off-limit surfaces the most enticing place in the world for Chester to be. And the envelope-pusher in him relishes these moments of blatant rule breaking.

I will never forget my first Christmas with Chester. Two things to note before I go any further: first, I love Christmas. Like seriously, I still have a hard time falling asleep on Christmas Eve and I am up at dawn on Christmas morning. Yes, I know I am an adult, and yes, I know Santa Claus isn't real. Second, Chester loves Christmas even more than I do.

I grew up celebrating the holidays around an artificial Blue Spruce-style Christmas tree and, as a result, we never had tinsel. As such, this particular Christmas I decided I would decorate a real tree and drape its boughs with silver tinsel. Chester thought that this was a fantastic idea also. This is when I found out how much he liked Christmas, too. No sooner did I have the tree lit and decorated before he dove into the fir face first. I worried that the tree would fall over, so I called my dad for ideas. Together we lashed the tree to the walls and the floor with cables and placed twenty pounds of weights on the tree stand for greater security and stability. The cat was not phased in the least bit.

When Chester slept, he slept under the tree. When Chester was awake, he was in, under, and on the tree. He literally ate, drank, and slept Christmas tree. I came home from work one evening to find pine needles strewn about *the entire house*. He chewed off all of the lower branches of the tree that he could reach at the trunk and dragged them all over the house. I think he thought that when he ran with the branches in his mouth, they were chasing him. I'm sure it was a super fun game. My role in the game, clean up, was not quite as fun.

Then it happened. The moment in every pet owners' relationship with their pets where they do something that they never thought they would ever, under any circumstances, find themselves doing. In my case, it was when Chester came to me with those big, loving eyes and asked me to pull the tinsel out of his bum. Yes, he, too loved the shiny tinsel, and I will never forget pulling piece after piece out of his behind. He winced. I winced. Needless to say, the tree didn't make it to Christmas day and I have never had a real tree with tinsel since.

All joking aside, I owe so much to this cat. This is probably about the point where you begin to think that I am a crazy cat lady (in case that thought hadn't already crossed your mind). Let me confess that I have two cats, Chester and Elliott. Most people tend to gravitate toward Elliott because he looks like a fluffy white bunny rabbit with his little pink ears and nose, but I have a bond with Chester that is inexplicable. To his credit, I don't think he realizes he isn't human. After all, I treat him like a human, so why would he think otherwise? I saved his life and in return he saved mine. He has truly been there for it all. He has been the one and only first-hand witness to this whole mess.

After heated arguments with my husband, he was always waiting for me. He let me bury my face in his furry belly and bawl. He would lick my forehead until I fell asleep. Every night, no matter what, Chester would watch over me, perched above my head or wrapped around me like a fur stole. He stood by silently as we married, and still loved me unconditionally afterwards, when I hated myself. He sat on top of the suitcase in the closet that night. In the nights that followed the divorce, he paced nervously until I returned home. If he could have held my hair out of the way while I was puking in the toilet, I'm sure he would have. If I slept on the bathroom floor, so did he. Right before I would burst into tears, he would come charging to my aid, rubbing his face in my hands, as if to say, "It's okay. It's all going to be okay. Please stop crying. Just pet me, and you'll start to feel better. I promise. Trust me. I trust you." And he always stands by my side willing to do whatever it takes to make me sane again. He has a sixth sense, at least when it comes to me.

He always looks over me and tries to protect me, the best a cat can.

To this day, Chester has an issue with suitcases. When he sees one, he instinctively does everything in his power to put at much fur on it as possible, as if to say, "Please don't go! Please don't leave without me, but if you must, please don't forget about me! I am giving you lots of fur to remind you of me and make you want to come home sooner." I get comments every time I go through security in the airport regarding the quantities of cat fur that is permanently woven into the suitcase fabric as a result of Chester's diligent efforts.

This is the deep, loving relationship I have with a cat. Yes, a cat. Even now, although he's filled out to 13.2 pounds and carries a nickname reminding him of that, he loves and supports me. As I dream up new business ideas or try to figure out how to implement current ones, he sits on the stool next to me in the kitchen. I bounce my ideas off him. If it sucks, he tells me so as indicated by his lack of reaction. So-so ideas warrant a flat, "Meh." Good ideas are rewarded by a hand nudge with his nose. Think I'm kidding? Ask around. When you work from home by yourself and have no one else to talk to except a pet, then call me and tell me I'm crazy. Suffice it to say that I love this dear little creature and am so grateful that he came into my life.

VIII

SEX, DRUGS & CLASSICAL MUSIC

"All the suffering, stress, and addiction comes from not realizing you already are what you are looking for"

JOHN KABAT ZINN

I wish I could tell you that it was just that easy. That I made my decision to end my marriage, stood my ground, walked away, and life turned around for me. In fact, I really don't want to tell you this next part. It would be easier to keep it to myself, but that wouldn't actually help me or you for that matter.

How would I expect you to trust me, let alone perhaps inspire something inside of you, if I wasn't completely honest with you? I wouldn't. I would be holding back still trying to protect my deepest, most intimate moments. The moments that really need to be shared with someone so I don't have to be so alone with them anymore and so you know you're not alone either. We all have these moments, and they must be shared so someone else out there knows where you have been and you can come together and hold each other's hands in support. That is the only way my eMolecule shines and the only way I can hope to help make yours shine too. You have been warned. This is ugly. This is deep. This is so personal and raw, so don't judge me. Please have some dignity and grace and let me be if you don't like what you read.

The truth is, making the decision to leave my husband wasn't easy. It was my second black Pontiac moment. That's what I call those really hard life decisions, where you stand on the edge and look over just to get a peek, to try and see how bad it really would be if you took one more step in the same direction and fell. *How hard would I fall?* When you look over the edge and the ravine or canyon or whatever it is that you look down is so far down that you can't see the bottom, those are black Pontiac decisions. If you take one more step, it will be your last. There will be no turning back after that. No more time to change your mind. It's done.

When I am faced with a black Pontiac decision, I know that I have one shot to make my choice. The worst part is, there is no right or wrong answer per se, just a different path and another set of consequences. Neither choice will lead you down an easy path. Yes, there might be a path of least resistance, but in the end, you will still have to face some adversity to get to where you are headed.

In this case, with my marriage, I knew that if I stayed, it would be at the expense of possibility and exploration. I would never have a chance to find out who I am or what I could become. I would always be hiding, trying to stay invisible. Inside, I would always be screaming and pounding my fists to get out and break away. Yes, we would have happy times and bad times; we'd already experienced some of those moments. Could I have been happily ever after? Perhaps. But it would be the fake happy. You know, the kind of fleeting guilty happiness you get when you fall in love with a must-have pair of shoes or scarf. You end up buying it because you are so happy in that moment, and then the inevitable guilt follows. The negative thoughts just compound one on top of the other. *Why did I just spend this much money? Where will I ever be able to wear this? I have nothing to go with this. You idiot! You knew this would happen. What were you thinking?!?*

Now, I don't mean to compare marriage or the demise of one to an impulse retail purchase, but we have all experienced that kind of dissipating happiness that can take place. Take that small amount of remorse and guilt and multiply it by one hundred and add fifteen pounds of the hardest soul-shaking grief you can muster. Feel that? That is what this black Pontiac decision felt like.

I broke his heart. And I did it intentionally. That was the consequence of my decision to not sacrifice getting to know me. It was either going to be him or me and I chose me. I can't say that I got away unscathed. My heart, which I had given away to him so fully and completely in the beginning, had been whittled down into little pieces. I'd given it to him because he promised to take care of it and protect it. Instead, he'd methodically shaved off little pieces, bit by bit, over the years until all I had left was pain and hurt and emptiness. I was worried I wouldn't have enough heart left over to ever love again or that there would be too much scar tissue to ever try to give my heart away again.

Nope. There was definitely no turning back on this decision. Once the dirty deed was done, it would be irrevocable.

This kind of decision eats at you. Before you've made it, while you're deciding, and after you've made it, the what-ifs haunt you. I felt hollow and more numb than any alcohol or drug induced state could make me. I was a zombie in the truest sense of an animated yet lifeless form. When you're here in this place, sleep is not an option. In fact, it feels like your enemy. Any time you are alone with your thoughts, it is your enemy. So to try to escape, you do whatever it takes for that little slice of peace and glimmer of pleasure because it certainly isn't happiness that you find when you're here. But these little moments are all you have to avoid the thoughts from flooding in and making you go crazy again inside your head. You have silence and fake bliss or you have deafening, maddening, and terrifying voices coming at you from a thousand different directions, making you insane. This is why you will do whatever it takes. I mean *anything*.

The decision to end my marriage led me down a dark path. I picture it like this: There is a dark storm on the horizon. It is a nasty storm. Bellowing thunder, blood curdling lightning, with wind so powerful it could strip flesh from bone. I could stay married, which would mean I could stand under partly cloudy skies waiting and watching the storm march toward me until it inevitably arrived. This would be the easier-for-now choice. Or, I could dive right into the heart of the storm, get beaten and battered, but it would continue to move and then I would be able to relax under partly cloudy skies hoping the worst had passed over. This would be the let's-eat-shit-now-and-hope-I'm-still-alive-when-it's-over choice. This is the choice I made and it almost killed me.

That storm cloud was bad, and it was vast. And I did whatever I could to survive. That was all I could do. Bravery was not an option. Cowardice was not an option. Surviving was enough. To silence the insanity in my head, I returned to my always-there-for-me-friend, alcohol, big time. Okay, so maybe this time alcohol wasn't enough and I snorted a little bit of cocaine here and there and dabbled in other drugs. I had come all this way from that damn car hood in Georgia, just to find myself right back where I started, but at least I didn't hurt. I was so fucked up; I couldn't feel anything. I'm not sure that I could have handled any feelings, good or bad. Anything would have sent me over the edge. I say that now, "edge," but I am pretty certain that I was already over the edge and really couldn't go much further.

The lowest point came right after the divorce. I stopped eating. Well, I guess that's actually a lie because I would show up for work at T.G.I. Fridays and eat one hardboiled egg and a package of two saltine crackers. I wasn't hung over yet, because I was still drunk and high from the night before. During the shift, I would spike my Diet Coke or Sprite. After work, I would drive (yes, I said drive) back to my apartment, snort or pop something while I got ready to go out to the bar, usually meeting up with fellow co-workers.

You see I led a double life. During the day, I was a mostly held together student that got good grades and had a part-time job. This came with a subset of familiar faces, but no one that I actually engaged with. I really didn't want them to get to know me and I certainly did not care to get to know them. Now, I would hang out after work with the restaurant faces. We'd go out to bars and drink heavily together. Then, during the late-late night, I would slide into the underbelly of society full of unfamiliar faces that I never wanted to remember and snort, swallow, or smoke anything I could. I never mixed crowds. EVER. This was my little dark secret that no one needed to know about, except for me. I was ashamed, but couldn't stop myself. I actually looked forward to the dark nights where I knew nobody, where I didn't have to talk to anybody, where I didn't have to pretend. There were no bullshit conversations about what I ate that day or what color I was thinking about dyeing my hair. I didn't have to feign interest in Justin Timberlake.

My apartment was an explosion of sequins, glitter, and high heels. It literally looked like a hooker might have exploded in there. Dirty clothes were piled with clean clothes and brand new clothes. Nothing in my life mattered. I squandered everything because everything was expendable: clothes, money, men, friends, and opportunities. The only concern I had was to keep myself from feeling anything at all. The moment I felt a twinge of a sober moment, I would fling myself at a bottle or baggie, diving into it like it was my last supper. Life was a blur, which was exactly the way I wanted it to be.

I was wild and rowdy. The wilder I was, the more accepted and "popular" I became. All the girls wanted to know how I dropped so much weight because I just looked fabulous now and so skinny. All the guys wanted to sleep with me because I seemed so fun and unpredictable. This makes no sense. My peers were encouraging me to do *this* to myself, casual sex, inebriation, intoxication.

This is wrong. I need help, but I can't stop.

I sat alone in an alley next to a bar on a milk crate. I stared down trying to focus on the bits and pieces of my now shattered cell phone but I couldn't get my eyes to focus. *Shit! My phone is broken.* My thoughts were preoccupied with my broken cell phone; like in this moment, a broken cell phone was the worst possible thing that could have ever happened. It was freezing cold outside. There were banks of snow piled around the corners of the buildings and grey frozen slush in the roads. I was wearing a red tube top with sequined trim and a mini skirt made of faded blue denim and my feet were bare. I had no idea where my shoes were. I should have been shivering, but I just stared blankly at my broken cell phone and my toenail polish.

A police cruiser pulled up along the entrance to the alley. I slowly turned my head, unable to keep my gaze straight. And in an instant upon recognition of the vehicle, my flight response involuntarily took over my body and I confusedly found myself running down the alley. My mind was telling me to stop, my heart was screaming at me to stop because it felt like it was going to explode trying to keep up with pumping my blood, but my flight response ignored the pleas from my body. I skirted through the spaces between the gates on a locked chain link fence, cutting my shoulder. Tears streaked down my face, as I tore through the snow barefoot. The frigid air seemed to cut my lungs with each gasping breath.

I looked back to find that no one had followed me, but I couldn't recognize where I now stood. The cold caught up to me. I noticed it first in the blistering hot pain that shot up from the soles of my feet. I looked around, trying to gain my bearings, but the pain was growing so intense it clouded my ability to concentrate. I made out the oncoming brightness from headlights coming down the street. I darted out into the street flailing my arms sporadically. As the lights drew nearer, I noticed the orange flashing light on the vehicle roof and made out the strong lines of a city snowplow. I could barely stand now, the pain in my feet was unbearable. The vehicle slowed. I presume the driver stopped to ask if I was okay and I may or may not have fumbled out a slurred response.

I awoke swaddled in blankets under the harsh brightness of hospital lighting. Someone had just left my room and then a doctor appeared. He began lecturing me about the perils of drugs and alcohol use and asking me questions about the previous night's events. I had no answers for him. I saw him talking, but couldn't hear him. I turned my head and closed my eyes. I couldn't deal with him right now and I wanted nothing more than to get the hell out of there as fast as possible. I turned my head again to face him, feigned a smile and frankly stated, "Thank you. I'm fine. I'm leaving now." I untangled myself from the blankets and placed my bare feet on the floor readying to stand.

"Holy shit! that f@#$ing hurts!" a voice inside my head screamed.

"Shhhhh. They'll make you stay here if you show weakness. Just grin and bear it," another voice chimed in.

I decided to listen to the second voice of reason, and again flashed a phony smile at the doctor as I steadied myself. The kind-looking middle-aged nurse pointed to my belongings on the chair and advised me that she would ready my discharge papers. I looked down at my feet to find them dressed and wrapped in bandages. I sighed in relief that they were both still there and swiftly changed back into my clothes. I tried to duck out unnoticed, but was caught by the pleasant nurse. She ushered me into a small office-like room while handing me a pair of socks and plastic booties. I became intensely aware of my clothing and lack of shoes. My cheeks flamed up in embarrassment and I was ashamed to look her directly in the eye. A counselor met us in the small office. He looked to be in his late-fifties and utterly exhausted, his forehead deeply creased from concern. He seemed compassionate enough and as though he genuinely wanted to help.

Yes, it would seem that I was another Jane Doe that had washed up on their doorstep and the only way they would let me leave was if I agreed to counseling. Like all good addicts, I definitely was fine and didn't need help. I had my life under control and rattled off some excuses about going through a "rough patch." Like good counselors, they didn't buy it.

Deep down I knew they were right, but I was nowhere close to admitting that to myself. I nodded my head as they rattled off warning signs and dangers of addiction. The nurse reminded me that I had been brought to the hospital after a municipal utility worker found me collapsed in the street. They pumped my stomach upon arrival and treated me for second and third degree frostbite on both feet and hypothermia. I had alcohol poisoning and a blood test revealed narcotics in my system. Ouch! Now that is a serious blow to anyone's ego. I was pissed that I let myself get caught.

While I was out partying all night long, I enrolled again for the upcoming semester. I didn't sign up for classes because I wanted to get my education. I didn't really care that much about getting a diploma. That was my mom's dream, not mine. What I cared about was subsidizing my lifestyle and foregoing any decisions that would make me accountable or responsible. The answer: stay in college. Since I had married, I automatically was considered an independent and my parents' income no longer had any bearing on my eligibility to receive financial aid. I qualified to receive a federal grant and a state grant to cover the costs of my schooling and living expenses. I signed up for college to take the money and run. But I needed help. I was back in place where no one should be, and I needed someone to catch me and pull me out. My angel came along, in the form of a college professor.

I really owe my "success" in college to the compassion of one of my professors. Although I never shared my story with him, I don't think I had to. I think he knew that I was in a dark place and needed help, but he saw more. He could see that my eMolecule was ablaze and all I needed to help coax it out was some direction. In fact, when I reached out to him to tell him

I was writing this book, I called his office line and was thankful to get his voicemail, but then realized that I hadn't practiced or thought of a voicemail message to leave. As I stumbled over my thoughts, my words went something like the following, "Hi, this is Mary Todd . . . errr, ummmm, I mean Mary Wolff. Uh, I graduated a while ago. I'm not sure if you remember me, but well, umm . . . . uh, call me back." He promptly returned my phone call and heartily chimed, "Like I wouldn't remember you, HA! We had some rough times there, huh?" *Aptly said, Professor, but rough is a bit of an understatement.*

As that semester was getting started, I reviewed my class schedule with disgust. None of the economics classes or Spanish classes appealed to me. They seemed hard. Too hard. I had already fallen back on my "safety net," staying just coherent enough to function without getting arrested. The voices in my head were getting louder. I think they were becoming immune to sedation by alcohol, but I couldn't afford all of the drugs in the world to keep them quiet.

I sat in my bathtub in my apartment. The water was hot, but I was shivering. Edward Elgar's *Enigma Variations* filled the air with palpable emotion. I stared at the paring knife I had pulled from the kitchen drawer and placed on the tub's edge. I picked it up and my heart raced faster, increasing tempo with the music. I placed the cold blade to my wrist and applied a little pressure, testing the waters. Once it broke past the resistance from my skin, the tip slid in easily, but it hurt. I pulled it back out and took another hearty pull off the tequila bottle, also stationed on the bathtub's edge. There were frantic meows and pawing from the other side of the door. I ignored them.

"What are you doing, Mary? If this is where you were going to end up, why did you bother even getting divorced? You just destroyed that man and this is how you respect him, how you respect the sanctity of that marriage?"

"NO! This isn't where I want to be, but I still don't know where I am going. I don't have the strength to keep walking. All I have been doing is walking. Walking endlessly and aimlessly. And for what purpose? It is just

a big circle. I am right back where I started. Help me . . . I don't want to be here, but I don't know what to do. I want this all to be over. I am done with this place. I want to move on, but I am scared. Why am I always scared?"

"What is there to be afraid of?"

"I don't know . . . Life I guess."

"Why be afraid of life? If you didn't want to live, you could have stayed in Georgia. You could have killed yourself or just disappeared. Why didn't you just do that? You still can."

"Because. Mary, you've been here before and you've never been able to follow through. Something is keeping you here. Something must matter if you are still here."

"Because what? There's nothing to be afraid of"

"Because I can't..."

"Why not? Are you afraid to die, too?"

I took several more chugs from the tequila bottle, strengthening my resolve. *"No! I'm not afraid. I'LL SHOW YOU!!!"* I picked up the paring knife again, haphazardly trying to get it to fall back into the previous cut. I felt it catch on the cut skin and slide back in; it sent a deep pleasure pain up my spine. It hurt, but it was also euphoric. My heart raced again with the tempo from the eighth variation of Elgar's composition. Then the music changed variations, switching to *Nimrod*. The tempo slowed and the melody swept over me. I looked down at the knife tip in my wrist and blood trickling down my arm and dripping into the bathwater. I started to weep. The music was so beautiful. It was inside me. It was telling me what a beautiful place this world was. And, that I was beautiful too. I threw the knife at the wall, disgusted with myself.

"What are you doing?"

"I can't do this."

"Coward!"

"I know! I am! BUT PLEASE! JUST LEAVE ME ALONE! I can't do this. I don't want it to be like this. I can't bear the thought of my family grieving for me. My parents would have so much guilt. They would always wonder where they went wrong. What they could have done differently. They

would blame themselves, but I would be the one to blame. I can't wrongfully condemn them to that fate. I cannot make them be a zombie like me. They have worked too hard; they have sacrificed too much. The thought of hurting my family is too much to bear. I am hurting them now, but I don't know how to stop. Help . . ."

When I woke up, I was laying naked in the bathtub covered in a mix of blood and vomit. The water had been drained. I must have kicked the drain lever or something. Chester, my best friend and cat, was sitting on the toilet waiting for me. When I roused, he perked up, sat up and meowed. He'd had a sleepless night waiting and watching to see if I would come to. I sat up and saw the knife on the travertine floor and the mark on the wall where the knife hit the plaster. I grabbed him in my arms and hugged him so hard, I'm surprised he didn't try to escape and that I didn't crush his little bones. I started wailing. Tears running hot down my cheeks. I was so grateful to be alive. I was pouring love out of every part of my body onto this cat. When I thought I had no one, he was there. *He needed me.* I sat in the bathtub and cried on Chester for the greater part of the morning. He didn't move and he didn't try to leave me. Maybe he was grateful I was still here, too.

Something needed to give. I wasn't going to make it out alive if something didn't change. I chose this path because I wanted to find myself; well find myself I must do then.

You need to put the divorce and the "old you" behind you. Today is a new day. You are alive. You have been given another chance. Don't fuck this up.

Something did give. I was different. I wanted to move on. For the first time in my adult life, I felt ready. Ready for what, who knows?

I picked up the brochure the counselor had given me at the hospital. I knew I'd missed three or so meetings already. I dialed the number hoping it wouldn't ring or there would be no answer. My voice cracked, "Um, hello?" I coughed to clear my throat. "We met a few weeks ago. I, er, uh, um." The gentle voice on the other end of the line stepped in to the rescue. "It's

okay. We'll see you on Thursday. You're always welcome here."
I was relieved that I didn't have to sit through another lecture or say anything more for that matter. This was the beginning of a whole new way of being.

I also decided that I was ready to be done with college once and for all. I wanted to leave this place and all the memories of it behind me. I had been in college on and off for three years now, and I wanted to pull the Band-Aid off as quickly as possible and get it over with. I longed for a fresh start to put my past behind me and let my future define me (well, sort of . . .). I scheduled a meeting with my college advisor to find out how I could get out of undergraduate school as quickly as possible so I could start my new life. Little did I know that meeting would in fact define my unknown (at the time) ambition.

"Hey, it's Mary. I'm here to discuss my options for graduation."

"Well, let's see your credit history . . . Oh! It looks like you have taken quite a range of classes over several programs of study at a few institutions. On your current major declaration, economics, it looks like you will have three more years of core class study left and you will be required to declare and complete a minor. So realistically, if you attended semesters consecutively *and* take summer school, you could expect to graduate in three and a half to four years."

"I see, but here's the problem with that: I have already been in college for three years. I just need to finish; like yesterday isn't soon enough. I can't do this anymore. I am DONE with college. With the classes I have taken so far, what major will get me out of here the fastest? I don't care what it is, I just need to get that stupid piece of paper so I can make my mom proud."

"Entrepreneurship."

"Entreeeewhat? I don't speak French." (Some food words, absolutely, duh! *a la mode?* Every time.) "Heck, I can't even speak Spanish despite taking Spanish classes for at least five years."

"You'll be done in two and a half years. It's the best you can do. You'll have to take one summer class or two to make up extra credits. This program does not require you declare and complete a minor either"

"Prefect. I'll do it." *Hmmmmm . . . I am going to be an entrepreneur. Awesome!* "So what exactly am I going to be studying?"

"Business."

"Okay, cool. I like business. Sign me up."

This short, completely ridiculous conversation would change the course of the rest of my life. It is this single word, *entrepreneur* that gave name to that little spark in me. I had just named my eMolecule. I *finally* fit in. Okay, let's be honest. I still didn't really fit in, so let's just say I finally found my niche. Quite by accident or happenstance or whatever. Call it whatever name you want, I have learned that it doesn't really matter because I found my path.

But as I said, there was one professor who recognized my potential. I wonder what it was he saw in me. I felt that I must have looked like a scared, scarred little mouse. Professor was a big, boisterous Texan. His voice boomed out with a Southern twang. He wore black cowboy boots with his trousers and his shirt was tucked neatly in his belt-buckle-clad waist. He was always smiling from ear to ear. You could tell Professor was really just a big ol' teddy bear, but by the same token, should you cross him . . . well, maybe he had been a gunslinger in his past life and you would find yourself in hot water before you even knew there was a pot on the stove. His classes were different. Instead of lecturing us, reading textbooks, and applying principles to issues, he told us stories and experiences from his life. He shared his path: the really awesome times and the times where he learned what he was made of. He was honest and heartfelt. He was my angel.

Two of his stories resonated with me, and still do because as he told them, you could see the emotions flicker across his face like, instead of recounting the tale, he was actually in the moment living it. It was painful yet simultaneously beautiful. Both stories are about love.

Back when Professor lived in West Texas and was involved in one of his many entrepreneurial adventures; he lived in a trailer with his family. I can hear him now: "Well, there are two things you need to know about West Texas to understand what I was puttin' my family through. First, there ain't nothing in West Texas except cattle and tumbleweed. Second, it's hot. *Really dang hot.*"

He was in the cattle trucking business and he was losing the shirt off his back. It wasn't going well. There were all sorts of issues. The first straw was when he found himself unloading and then reloading cattle into the back of a semi-truck trailer in the middle of the night in the summer just sweating his fanny off because the first semi-truck broke down. Shortly thereafter, the air conditioning broke in the family's trailer, "and IT was HOT! God bless my wife though, 'cause she never complained." But Professor could not bear to see his wife so graciously sit in the trailer without complaint, just sweating all the time. She looked miserable and exhausted. This was the final straw. He knew something had to give. He needed to change his course so his family would not have to suffer his mistakes, too. So he did. Just like that.

Wow! He's fearless. I want to be like that. I want to own my own future. I decide what goes, I decide what happens next.

The second story is about his son. Professor's son was a drug addict and it almost cost his son's life. His son stole from his parents and did whatever it took to get his next fix. I could relate to that part, but it's the next part, the part I never really considered, that struck home. I knew what my life looked like from my perspective, but I never really tried to see it from a parent's perspective. Just as his son did whatever it took to get his fix, Professor did whatever it took to get his son back; property was mortgaged, business interests were sold. It almost bankrupted the family, but Professor refused to give up on his son. His son went in and out of rehab; there were relapses. It cost the family a fortune in dollars and an untold amount of love and heartache, but he got his son back. Professor was able to save one of the most prized parts of his life, his child, and admits that had if he'd not been able to bring his son home, it would have destroyed both his life and his marriage.

This second story made me realize how close I really was to destroying everything. I almost had, but there still was a long way to go to rebuild it all. But *I* could do this. I continued that semester with a renewed zeal for life. Instead of just going through the motions or merely showing up, I began to engage. I engaged the people around me, with my classmates, and most importantly, with myself. My entrepreneurship classes turned out to be the perfect blend of business know-how, creativity, and self-study to suit my newfound motivation. More importantly, I realized that the rickety old bridge in the jungle leading home had always been there. In fact, on second glance, it is made of stone, solid and safe. It even has lights so I can find my way home in the dark. I went home and got reacquainted with two of my best friends, my parents. And yup, you guessed it. They were waiting for me with open arms. They didn't care what I had done, where I had gone, or what happened. They were so grateful just to hold me in their arms again, to have me back.

So, I can't imagine that Professor knew all this about me when I first walked into his classroom, but maybe he did. Maybe I had that same look in my eyes that he had seen in his son's eyes or perhaps the angels were telling him that I needed to be brought back home because my parents needed someone's help to bring me home, since they couldn't reach me. Whatever the case may be, it worked and I am forever grateful.

IX

THOUGHTS ON ENTREPRENEURSHIP

"Our deepest fear is not that we are inadequate;
Our deepest fear is that we are powerful beyond measure"

MARIANNA WILLIAMSON

By the time I finally graduated with my undergraduate degree, I had attended five colleges and universities and had declared a different major ten times. One of my declared majors was even "student-at-large." I cannot tell you what that program of study entails, but I would say that it probably was the description that best fit my speckled and disjointed collegiate path. (I should point out that as I write this, Pandora has decided to play *Pomp & Circumstance* on my classical music station. How astute, Pandora! For once, you are not playing a song that is a head scratcher . . . *how did we go from Jimmy Buffet to Foo Fighters?*)

But that's just it; it didn't matter what my path was or how long it took me to get there. The point is that *I got there* because I *never stopped walking.*

You know, a lot of people ask me, "Why did you stay in school?"

My response: "Why not?" The truth is it was the only thing keeping me connected. When everything else was falling apart around me, I still had school. It (mostly) didn't matter if I showed up or not. I didn't have to answer to school the same way one has to answer to a boss. School didn't care or judge me. Also, I was good at school. I always had been. So even if I was failing in all other aspects of my life, I still did well in school. I could sleep easy knowing that I was at least doing one thing (sort of) right. Well, and that another reason: money.

What did I get out of it, finally? Yes, that little piece of paper I showed my mom proved that her sacrifices were worth it. But I got to put a name with a face, so to speak. I was given a safe space to learn and practice and to scratch the tip of the iceberg of self-awareness. I could look in the mirror and recognize the girl that was looking back at me. She didn't know where she was going yet, but she looked confident that she was going some- where big.

What I love about entrepreneurship is that there are no lim- its or rules. I don't seem to operate well in a world with lots of rules or taking orders from someone telling me how to get things done. That isn't to say rules are wrong, bad, or meant to be broken, but I do better with simple guidelines. Rules seem to indicate that there is a right way and a wrong way. For God's sake, I've done many things wrong, but that doesn't mean that I don't get my fair shot at happiness, does it? No. It doesn't work like that.

Guidelines are more like a road map. You have a destina- tion and the map (guidelines) show you different ways to reach your destination, but you get to choose how to get there. This is entrepreneurship. *You get to choose.* There are, of course, over- arching principles that just spell good business, but there isn't a secret no-fail formula. I have learned that there are a few special ingredients that make a huge difference when it comes to your likelihood of achieving success, but more on that later.

I am also a huge fan of fresh starts. Entrepreneurship lets you come up with whatever you want to be and you can start over as many times as you like. But again, you get to choose. You get to be the holder of your future. You decide.

This was so foreign to me at the time. Why is it that we force kids and adults, even, into defining *what* they are? And if we do force definitions onto people, why is it always in terms of a specific job or job function? Even worse, dependent on the answer provided, that person will be judged on so many levels: income, intelligence, upbringing, happiness and so on and so forth. These are assumptions! We judge and decide without ever actually learning the whole story.

If I told you I was a teacher, how would you perceive me? You would probably assume that I make approximately $30-$50K a year and that I like kids. If I told you I was a lawyer, how would you perceive me? You would assume that I have boatloads of money, my life is some television series saga of power suits, dramatic court appearances, and I have a sweet ride. Well, screw that! All of it! I say, if you are an elementary school teacher, you tell people that you are inspiring the next generation of leaders. Why? Because that demonstrates your passion, and passion is one of those secret ingredients I just mentioned, and it shows people who you are, not what you merely do.

So I challenge you to also change your question. The next time you meet someone for the first time, don't ask the predictable "What do you do?" as a means of determining who that person is, but ask "Who are you?" I know who I am. Do you know who you are?

In my opinion, regardless of career field, entrepreneurship is the very thing will help fuel our economy for future generations. Yes, I predict there will always be traditional companies out there, but it will be from harnessing our eMolecules and starting businesses that combine our passions with just a bit of business savvy. We will not only have a more secure financial future, but we will actually make the world a better place. Innovators in their industries will be the ones like Atlas, carrying our world forward on their shoulders. Okay, that's enough. I'm getting off my soapbox now.

So you're no doubt wondering if I got all of this from an entrepreneurship degree? Yes. I used those educational tools coupled with my life experiences. I was always running away from labels, afraid to define myself because I didn't want to be typecast by other people in my own life. I should get to choose, right? Or worse, what if I chose incorrectly? Now I have a label, but it means anything I decide it means. Does it provide a false sense of security? Yeah probably, but at least I am aware and conscious of that. And even better, I can decide when I want to change labels. Entrepreneur might be good for today, but tomorrow, maybe I'll tell people I'm a writer. Who knows?

With my entrepreneurship education, I wasn't told how to get from point A to point B. Instead, I was instructed to just get there. Ideas and ingenuity were rewarded, not punished. I thrive in this type of environment. Believe it or not, most people thrive in this type of environment, but this is the exact opposite of many work environments. What keeps people in that environment? Fear. And I understand that too. I know A LOT about fear. I was fortunate enough to get to learn how to ride the entrepreneurship bike with training wheels on and in a supervised padded room. Nothing hinged on my ideas except grades, so it really didn't matter. What mattered was that I got to explore. I had permission to explore myself, discover problems, and come up with solutions. I had permission to have fun trying to define something new or to come up with wacky ideas just for the sake of fun.

One of these silly ideas was a topless hair salon hypothetically set in Wrigleyville in Chicago, Illinois. I named it "A Little Off the Top." For one whole semester, I got to plot and plan this business like it was the real deal. I knew it certainly wasn't anything I would actually pursue, *but it was fun.* Something crazy happened with that silly idea, too. A journalist for the local newspaper picked up my idea. The article opened with "Illinois State University senior Mary Wolff (my name at the time) reached a fork in her career path: law school or topless hair salon." If that doesn't make a mother proud . . . Hey, I was runner-up in the ISU business plan competition that year, only to be beat out by my good friend who actually planned on pursuing his business venture, which he did and did so quite successfully, I might add.

Turns out, I really excel at planning. I am a visionary who can see the big picture, step back and plan the details on how to get there. While going through the planning process for this hypothetical venture, my classmates respected me. I impressed them with my casual conversations about my ideas, in my formal presentations, and in my comprehensively laid out business plans. I became a go-to resource and sounding board for my peers. When they got stuck with something in their own venture planning (or life), they came to me to help problem-solve and generate ideas.

"What? You mean you want my help? HA! You do realize that I am two steps shy of going off the deep end at any moment and that I am a wild card—not in a good winning the card game way, but more in the super-risky undependable way."

"SHHHHHH! I'm trying listen to what the problem is."

"Wait until they find out what you've done. They won't come to you anymore. They'll realize you don't know anything. You have lots of problems that you can't seem to solve. What makes you think you can help them troubleshoot their problems?"

"I already told you to SHUT UP! I can do this. I am doing this. Don't believe me? Watch me! Watch me kick ass and blow this out of the water!"

"Whoa! Since when did I start taking charge over the voices in my head? Wait, what? I can control the voices of doubt and fear? This is awwww-wesome!"

Slowly but steadily, my studies helped me build self-confidence because I found something that fed me internally. I discovered my eMolecule. It had been there all along guiding me, but I was afraid to acknowledge it and do something undefined. I was intentionally suppressing my entrepreneurial spirit because I thought it was against the rules to harness it and, thus, the wrong choice to get me from point A to point B.

In times when I really needed something to happen, like when I was struggling to stay afloat in Chicago, my eMolecule came to the rescue. I didn't have a choice to harness it or not. It was a survival instinct surfacing up from the depths of me to provide for my family and for me. If it can rescue me in times of need, why did I keep trying to send it away? Fear. Self-doubt. You know, all those nagging little voices in your head that tell you, "you can't do it."

Well, I was finally starting to realize that I knew more than I gave myself credit for, that I could truly and honestly be anything I could dream up, and I was now armed with the education and tools to get me there. That's when I began to understand the power that I had inside of me, the possibility. That's when I began to understand the eMolecule.

PART TWO

X

GEOFFREY

"There's nowhere you can be that isn't where you're meant to be."

JOHN LENNON

As a child, our family was fortunate enough to take summer vacations to the beach. Oh, how I loved everything about the beach: the coarse, hot sand between your toes and underfoot, the salty ever-present breezes off the ocean, the abundance of curly, colored seashells, the soothing rhythm of the waves breaking on shore, and the call of seabirds floating with the clouds. I could spend hours at a time building sand castles, while my sister explored the ocean bottom with a pair of goggles. Mom always had a book in hand and would sneak in little naps on the beach. Dad split his time between helping me build architectural masterpieces in the sand, flipping my sister off his shoulders in the water, and teaching us both how to body surf in the waves. We all loved the beach, especially me. Being on the salty seacoast is my Dad's happy place, and I am truly a daughter after his own heart, because it is my happy place, too. In my mind, it was always a safe, warm place where I could escape whatever predicament I was currently in. I always had the beach.

I vowed at a young age that someday, when I grew up, I'd

know I had "made" it when I could wake up every morning and see a palm tree swaying outside my bedroom window, and I could walk on the beach whenever I wanted. If there ever was a constant dream throughout my life, this is the one: to live as close to the beach as possible, to lap up as many salty breezes and melting sunsets as I could in my lifetime. After graduating college, my resolve to make this a reality was unshakable. Come hell or high water, I was moving to Florida to live by the beach. It was nonnegotiable.

In my quest to make this happen, I went to Florida to visit prospective law schools. I was sitting in a chair outside a bar with friends in St. Petersburg, Florida when *he* spotted me. I was wearing an olive green tank top, a white skirt and had a black satin ribbon tied around my neck. I was reveling in the sun's setting rays, soaking up as much golden radiance as I could. I had spent so much time in darkness, all I longed for now was warmth and light.

As the man approached, I felt his eyes on me. I shifted uncomfortably in my chair and averted my gaze to avoid making eye contact. He was slim, but had a muscular frame. His skin was tanned from the sun, but his hair remained a dark brown, which he kept cropped close to his head and spiked up in the front. He struck me as borderline J.Crew with his royal blue pique polo, green cargo shorts, and beige Sperry Top Siders. He was casual yet preppy and pulled together. He was so wildly attractive, I immediately decided he was either (a) taken or (b) a total jerk. Either way, I had no business being with a man like that and forced myself to seem completely indifferent to the entire situation, but my heart was pounding nervously and with excitement in my chest.

Why is he looking at me?

When he reached the table, we exchanged glances and hellos. His name was Geoffrey. I was immediately enamored.

God, why did you have to make him so handsome?

Throughout the evening he tried to strike up conversations

with me. He was gentle, polite, funny, and so completely interested in me. I panicked from his attention. I wasn't used to getting attention from men, especially not really good ones, like
Geoffrey. So I handled the situation with the grace and panache
of an ogre. I tried to ignore him. I suppose I thought that if I
closed my eyes or ignored him, he would go away so I wouldn't
feel so uncomfortable in my own skin. To emphasize my disin-
terest, I ordered another round of drinks and slices of key lime
pie on his tab. I don't recall being particularly pleasant to him.

Instead of thoroughly enjoying the sweet moments of the
initial encounter with my future husband, I was wrapped up
in my thoughts. I pounded myself for not being good enough
for this man's attention and created a story that vilified him to
justify my righteousness. This internal dialogue manifested itself
outwardly through my snarky comments. Man, it was hard work
to stay hidden behind the self-created story. At each mean inter-
ruption I heard myself make, I wanted to jump out from behind
the self-imposed screen, pleading to this handsome man that it
wasn't really me talking. I don't actually say rude stuff like this.
I'm just nervous.

I suppose you could say Geoffrey brought out the worst in me
that night. I didn't show my true self because I was scared to put
myself on the line to risk possible rejection. I, instead, chose to
stay safely hidden behind the story I had created, so that if he
never called me, I could sit back and snarkily tell myself, "I told
you so." I was mortified.

Part of me wanted the night to end so I could save as much
face as possible, but the other part of me wanted it to last forever. I liked being around him. As the evening wound down, I left
that night and never looked back.

He called his mom that night and exclaimed that he'd just
met the girl he was going to marry.

Shortly thereafter, I hopped on a plane and moved to New
Zealand.

XI

LIVIN' IN A LAND DOWN UNDER

"Each of us must confront our own fears, must come face to face with them. How we handle our fears will determine where we go with the rest of our lives. To experience adventure or to be limited by the fear of it."

JUDY BLUME

My first "professional" job after I graduated took me to the other side of the world, literally. I moved to Christchurch, New Zealand, consulting for a Kiwi company that was looking to partner its logistics tracking technology and composite fabrication technology with an agricultural company in Illinois that was searching for new uses for the waste by-product from ethanol production, which in case you were wondering, is called dried distillers grains or DDGs. I received this opportunity in large part from my angel professor. He believed in me . . . and I was actually starting to believe in myself, too.

Remember how I told you I am a big fan of fresh starts? Well, this is the ultimate of ultimate fresh starts. First, I definitely did not know anyone who lived in New Zealand and the likelihood of running into a skeleton from what I now called my "past life" was pretty slim to zero. Second, I worked on a team with other young graduates who knew nothing about me, except that I had earned a Bachelor's degree in Entrepreneurship, and I hailed from a place called Normal, Illinois. We were tasked with creating a strategic plan for the joint venture and everyone brought a different educational and experiential background to the party.

It became very clear at the outset that my entrepreneurial studies were the most well-suited for this format. I had written business plans and strategic plans during my studies. I had even presented these plans to executives and financiers. I had the process and format down. As such, I emerged as the leader and expert with the team looking to me for guidance and task delegation. My eMolecule was burning strong, like an unquenchable thirst that I didn't care to get rid of, helping me push my own intellectual borders and the borders of physics with new, exciting ideas for DDG composite materials that might actually become a reality. I blossomed right there at that table in that conference room on Gasson Street, right before everyone's eyes. I transformed from a student into a leader. I no longer was a moth fighting for my chance at the flame, but a butterfly leading the way to flower pastures. I was creating the future not only of a new era for this company, but for myself.

Each day at the office my confidence grew, resulting in a newfound comfort and ease in my own skin. I looked in my bedroom mirror after work one day. Instead of seeing a scared, lost kid, I saw me: a beautiful, intelligent woman who was finally beginning to embrace and strut down her path instead of running and hiding from its inevitability, instead of kicking and screaming out of fear.

You used to be so scared. HA! Look at you now. You live on the other side of the globe. You were brave enough to take those steps. Not everyone would be. Look at what you can accomplish when you believe in yourself. You are well liked. You are looked up to. Company executives look at you as their peer, not some stupid kid. They are impressed by your outgoingness, your poise, your ingenuity, and your professionalism. Holy shit! That's you! You are amazing.

But this newfound confidence didn't come without a struggle. This was the first time I was really testing myself outside of my comfort zone. I felt alone and isolated. This was real. I wasn't trapped in my mind, there was no story to create, no excuses to make. I was alone. I essentially knew no one. Yes, I had been alone before, but there has always been a safety net: home. I had always stayed relatively close to home. There had always been the possibility of being rescued by my family. New Zealand really became a place for me to find my feet and learn how to stand on them. I was learning how to stand in my own skin.

I began to take my new confidence and apply it outside of the workplace. I was engaging. I was taking risks and rather enjoyed it, the rush of adrenaline, the twinge of self-doubt that crept up just a little too late to talk me out of it. I was becoming an adrenaline junkie; it was my new way to get high and it was exhilarating—the heavy, fast pounding of my heart, the quickening of my breath and then just going for it. It was as if I was beating the snot out of my "old self," showing her that instead of cowering in the face of fear, laughing was a much better choice. I was finally able to start setting myself free, physically and mentally. I hesitated at first, but the more I adventured, the less I hesitated.

Oh, and I did it all: bungee jumping, sky diving, canyoning, white water kayaking, black water rafting in caves, repelling down waterfalls, wrangling freshwater eels with my bare hands (which by the way I suck at), and exploring geothermal beaches and sulfuric "gardens." I even jumped off Auckland's version of the Seattle Space Needle. That one was actually the scariest. I don't care who you are; looking off the edge of a skyscraper and seeing nothing but the twisted metal and concrete of the city below, and knowing you are about to plunge right into the thick of it is enough to send anyone's heart right up into their throat. I earned my proudest achievement while staring my fears in the face: my Certificate of Fearlessness. Yes, me. I have achieved the impossible: I have proven that I am fearless even if it is only a mass produced piece of paper that some ticket clerk wrote my name on with magic marker. I don't care. That part doesn't matter to me. What matters is that I got a token, a physical token, to show the world that I, Mary Todd, have conquered the deepest, darkest thing in the world—fear. I could stare fear down and laugh at it. *HA! Take THAT!*

Okay, so I am not 100 percent fearless, it's true. I am not completely cured. You will learn, if you haven't already, that your path to finding and harnessing your eMolecule is fraught with fear. Once you overcome one fear, there is another one to takes its place, and another. It is a vicious and endless cycle. So if the fear never completely goes away, what do you do? You decide to not let it stop you. You decide that in spite of and to spite fear, you will move forward. Why? Because it is better than going backwards. So when you stop to catch your breath, you will realize what you just accomplished. Your confidence will grow just like mine did, and the next thing you know, instead of cowering in fear's presence, you will act, you will experience life, and those experiences are what define and create your unique self and your story. You will learn that the other side of fear isn't nearly as scary as you thought it was going to be. You will realize that you are stronger and braver than you ever could have imagined.

I was able to climb mountains and stand at the edge of the Earth. I know what it sounds like to be there, how it smells. It has left an indelible imprint on me. I can still hear the hissing sound of the retreating waves of the Tasman Sea on the beach of tiny, perfectly smooth pebbles. The brisk feel of the air from a squall rising up from Antarctica; the taste of the salty, frothy sea spray in my mouth; the smell of the lush and vibrant flora surrounding me on the cliff on the skirts of the southernmost rainforest in the world. I saw wild penguins migrating over rock formations that had once been part of the topography of the ocean floor, which are now visible in our current Cenozoic era. I was there. I experienced that. It forever changed me.

XII

ME? A LAWYER? HA!

"Whether you think you can, or you think you can't - you're right."

HENRY FORD

I returned stateside just in time to start law school. I was heading to Northern Illinois University's School of Law. I drove up there with friends and signed the lease on an apartment. I left my past behind and was ready to begin marching forward. A few days later, I found out that my ex-husband had just enrolled at NIU to complete his bachelor's degree.

I didn't despise him or anything at this point, but I couldn't be derailed. We were toxic to each other. I had worked so hard and come so far from my dark days of the past. I even journeyed halfway around the world to distance myself from my past. I could not take any chances and risk falling prey to the same temptations and mistakes.

I had gotten accepted to several other law schools, but had formally declined enrollment, except to one: Saint Louis University School of Law. Funny how I'd left myself an out without even realizing I would need one. Instead of heading north, I changed course and steered south, scrambling to get organized and set up in St. Louis, Missouri, before classes began in less than two weeks.

Before we go any further, I know you are questioning me right now. Didn't I just want to be done with school? The truth is yes, I wanted to be done with college, but that little annoying thing called fear, crept back up into my life. I now had this degree and master plan to become an entrepreneur. I was going to start my own business, or was I? I was scared. Really scared. I didn't have any business ideas, certainly no brilliant ones. Everything I had learned in business school about entrepreneurs pretty much fit into two categories: (1) great business ideas sprang up from people in the industry with lots of experience who had identified a problem and created a solution or (2) highly intelligent innovators came up with novel ideas related to technology. This coupled with the bottom line that 9 out of 10 businesses fail mantra that was hammered into me left me feeling a little bittersweet at graduation. YAY! I had my whole bright future ahead of me and I can do anything, BUT I still faced the eternally nagging question: *What am I going to do?*

Again, in my mind I played it safe. I would stick with what I knew and school is what I knew how to do. I feared that if I jumped too quickly into the real world, I would have a relapse of epic proportions. I quickly justified my decision by creating the rationale that business owners certainly must need to know about the law. Further, based on my speckled past, I may have run-ins with the law, so I would certainly garner some use and practicality out of going to law school. Finally, lawyers are expensive, so why not become one so I don't have to pay for one in the future. It was settled. Decision justified. I'm going to go to law school so I can start a business and not have to pay for a lawyer. Done.

Why exactly I thought this reasoning was sound I can't remember. And in case you are wondering, unless you plan on incurring $250,000 in upfront legal fees, it's probably cheaper to just pay for an attorney. When all of this is said and done and I finally pay off my student loans, I believe I will have paid approximately $1.4 million in "legal fees." Dang! Hindsight is always 20/20. HA!

What I do remember with perfect-detail-like-it-happened-yesterday clarity was telling my parents. I was sitting with them on their back deck, sipping a small glass of wine which inevitably and invariably is always accompanied by a tray of crackers, queen Spanish olives, and Cabot low-fat white cheddar cheese (the hummus and veggies are optional). We continued with the typical small talk: the weather, the recent warm up, work. I kept cool, although on the inside I was a ball of self-doubt. Then it happened: the questions about my future. What was I going to do? Had I been applying to jobs? What were my friends doing? I choked down my cracker, immediately regretting the decision to eat it in the first place. With my throat dry, I took a couple of big nervous gulps of my wine before croaking out a few indiscernible words. Mind reeling and heart racing, I started over, blurting out, "I'm going to law school."

The response I got was pretty much the same scene Elle Woods in *Legally Blonde* got from her parents:

"Law school, honey?"

"It's a perfectly respectable place, daddy."

"But law school is for boring serious people, and you, Button, are surely none of those things."

Okay, so my dad wasn't sipping a martini in a cable-knit sweater vest and my mom didn't look like a washed-up Barbie, but the level of disbelief was right on par. Who was I kidding? After all, it did take me five and a half years just to get through undergraduate school. Their perceived doubt in me was pretty well placed. But as any headstrong yet scared individual, I held my ground and played up the practicalities of going to law school, not to mention the prestigious notions of being a licensed professional. *Me? A licensed professional?* That still makes me laugh when I sit and think about it. Even if I never started my own business, I would still be a lawyer. It was a complete win-win.

And just like that, the next chapter in my journey unfolded. I felt safe and secure again, able to confidently state my future plans. Peers looked at me with awe; adults felt they had finally reached through to me to pursue my potential. I was steadfast and confident . . . until I showed up to law school at St. Louis University. It was a last-minute whirlwind decision, race to get an apartment, and to enroll in a different-than-planned school in less than two weeks, but I made it. I could breathe and rest.

I had thought that some of the people I'd met as an undergrad student were driven and had unwavering insight into what they wanted to be when they grew up. Well, that was until I found myself in a social mixer with my future 1Ls, that's code for first year law students, on the eve of the first day of classes. Everyone I talked to had wanted to be a lawyer since childhood. In fact, they gave me strange looks when I explained that I came to law school because I wanted to start a business and not pay a lawyer. I got even stranger looks when I revealed that a year ago, being an attorney hadn't even popped up on my radar. My heart raced as I continued making impersonal small talk through pursed lips and forced smiles. I became self-conscious that these people could see right through me. *Would they know that I was an addict? Does that disqualify me from being here? Someone else is probably much more deserving of my spot in class.* I was unable to answer seemingly simple questions.

"What Section are you in?"

"Uh, I don't know. How can you tell?" I asked, biting my bottom lip.

"What professor do you have for Torts? Civ Pro?"

"Ummm, I'm sorry, what's a tort?" I stammered back.

I had officially entered EgoTown where the population truly speaks with a sharp silver tongue, but their tongues were not nearly as sharp or stealthy as the silver daggers they would gladly, without hesitation or remorse, plunge into your back for self-gain and glory. I was waaaaaay out of my league and horribly unprepared. That's when I met Meghan.

I was standing outside the Career Services Office inside the law building, clearly looking lost. Meghan approached me and introduced herself. She started with the inevitable "what section are you in" conversation, and I braced myself for impact after answering that I had no idea. Instead of scoffing at me as though I were an idiot, as most of my fellow classmates had, Meghan asked to see my schedule. I cautiously produced a crinkled piece of paper scribbled with highlighter.

"You're in Section Six," she said with one glance at it.

"How do you know?"

"Because we have the same schedule and I'm in Section Six."

I immediately liked Meghan, but I was more in awe of her confidence and self-assuring personality. Meghan, like the others in law school, knew exactly where she was headed and how to get there.

Together, we walked into the Career Services Office. Meghan and I were greeted by a smiling woman in her sixties named Colleen. Colleen is my height with short brown curly hair and perfectly applied coral lipstick that matches the exact shade of her impeccable manicure. She has a deep, raspy voice like Lauren Bacall. Like Miss Bacall, Colleen could seamlessly slide into a Cadillac convertible, don a silk scarf tied around her head, and breeze by with her cigarette smoke glamorously curling around her coral clad lips. Aside from having Golden Age Hollywood glamour, Colleen is one of those individuals who hugs strangers as though she has known them for years and immediately makes even the most nerve-stricken person feel right at home and relaxed. Colleen became my mom-away-from-home and friend, letting me sneak diet Coke from the staff refrigerator or bringing me in simsimea, little round Middle Eastern treats made from dates or honey, sesame seeds, and spices.

Meghan and I sat in one of the interview rooms and chatted about the start of this next chapter in our lives. This is also where our friendship began. Meghan is my best friend. She is one of those ridiculously beautiful and perfect individuals who you really want to hate, but just can't because they're so down to earth and genuine. She is tall, with an athletic, but with a curvy frame that could have landed her a coveted spot in a Victoria's Secret catalog or on a runway, but instead she decided to go to law school because not only is she beautiful, she is insanely smart. This is one of those times I wish I were from Boston so I could say she is "wicked smaht," but alas, my Midwestern upbringing leaves me with no discernible sign of any sort of geo-locating accent. Ugh. Maybe in my next lifetime. And, as if that isn't enough, she is a top-notch athlete and one of the most level-headed, practical, and driven individuals I have ever met. She is my soul sister, despite the fact that she outshines me in pretty much every aspect.

Meghan defines the term "go-getter." I mean, heck, the term may have been invented just for her. When she decides to do something, she sees it through to the end, no matter what. Take for example when she decided to run a marathon. At the time, I could barely huff and puff through three miles at half her speed. I have since toyed with the idea of doing a half marathon, but reality quickly sets in and I laugh at myself for even having the thought in the first place. But not Meghan. Approximately twenty miles into her marathon run (which I feel ridiculous saying because I cannot even imagine running for twenty miles), she fractured her foot on an uneven portion of the pavement. Does Meghan stop? Nope. Does she walk the rest of the way? Nope. Does she slow her pace, limp, gimp, or hop her way to the finish line? Definitely, not. *Who does that?* Meghan. Permission to drop your jaw in awe granted. Can I see myself breaking my foot if I ever found myself in the unlikely scenario of running a marathon? Yes, but mine would be an intentional break about three to four miles in, so I would have a "legit" reason to quit.

Meghan is just amazing. She can pull off the seemingly impossible with such effortlessness. Well, at least that is what it looks like on the outside. The truth is, she works hard, really, really hard, every single day. I have days, my favorite sort of days that I call "hotel days." Hotel days are days where I lay in bed all day with no guilt and use the least amount of effort humanly possible to stay alive. The curtains stay closed, and I drift in and out of sleep catching bits and pieces of daytime television. Sometimes I curl up around a book. Whatever goes. That's the beauty of a hotel day. There is absolutely no cooking on these days. Delivery please. I have attempted to train the cats to order Chinese delivery, but we haven't progressed that far yet. I'm not sure if Meghan could handle a hotel day, at least not as often as I like to take them. She is constantly on the go.

If you are old enough, maybe you can remember back to Gatorade's "Be Like Mike" advertising campaign where undoubtedly the audience is reminded of its own deficiencies and how much sweeter life is for Michael Jordan. Although I am a huge Michael Jordan fan, the chances of me being a pro-WNBA-er are slim, I morphed this iconic marketing campaign to fit my more realistic expectations: *I want to be like Meghan* (in a completely non-creepy, totally healthy friend sort of way).

Throughout law school Meghan taught me so much about life and health. I am sort of the opposite of an athlete. I still close my eyes and wince when I go to catch a ball because I operate under the assumption that regardless of my best intentions to catch said ball, I anticipate that it will make contact with my forehead instead of my hands. To say I was stressed while in law school is an understatement. I can say with substantial certainty that my classmates also felt the strain. In the past when faced with stress, I would inevitably turn to alcohol to alleviate my "symptoms." Meghan taught me about the wonderful stress-relieving properties of exercise. I followed her to the gym three times a week and did the best I could to keep up. Not only did the gym provide a healthy outlet to relieve stress, but we also got to know each other better.

Meghan also kept me disciplined with my studies. Previously in college, I was fortunate enough to get good grades and succeed (by external standards) by putting forth minimal effort.

Law school was different. I actually had to learn how to apply myself, which comes with a significant learning curve. Actually having to read a textbook and be prepared for class was a total mystery. She taught me how to prepare and self-study through the use of flash cards (which are now my favorite study tool) and outlines. So thank you Meghan for helping me not to fail out of law school. I'd like to think that I provided something useful for Meghan during our three years in law school together, but nothing extraordinary comes to mind. Maybe just being her buddy was enough.

So you might expect someone with Meghan's traits to flaunt all of this, but she doesn't. For her, it's just business as usual and nothing out of the ordinary.

XIII

LAWS OF LOVE

"You know you're in love when you can't fall asleep because reality is finally better than your dreams."

DR. SEUSS

It was evident after a few weeks into the semester that, despite my friendship with Meghan, I didn't belong in law school. I was not cut from the same cloth as my classmates. I sought refuge in the Career Services Office.

This office became my safe haven and crutch for moral support to keep moving forward. I would check in with Colleen in the mornings and throughout the day, moan about a few classes and get the scoop on administrative drama. If I didn't show up for "check in," they would get worried that I'd just decided to call it quits. In this office, four individuals who barely knew me placed unrelenting faith in my future success. They nurtured me and cared for me. Helped me brush off the dirt and get back out there. This was also the place where I received not surprising news, but crushing all the same. I faced a legitimate turning point that would, like the unknowing decision to select entrepreneurship as my undergraduate major, define me. This, however, was a painful and conscious decision.

Three weeks into law school, I entered the Career Services Office, plopped down in a chair across from my confidante and career advisor, Anne, and blurted out, "I'm not supposed to a be a lawyer."

"Why do you think that?"

"Because I'm not like everybody else."

"Do you think all lawyers are the same?"

"Apparently."

"No, you don't actually think that. There are lots of differ-ent people that become lawyers and lots of different paths that are open to attorneys. Many people don't even practice law, but getting a legal education opens up doors. And don't think you are the first person ever to sit in that chair and tell me you don't belong here," she began.

Anne is extremely intuitive and perhaps the most graceful person I know. She is tall and slender with a fairy-like complex-ion, creamy white skin and short, pale pixie-blond hair. She looks like she was a model in her earlier years. Everything she does is with intention and awareness. Anne seems to epitomize peace and balance, long before I ever considered applying lofty principles like that to my life. Her calm silently coaxes out the self-doubt and worry and lays down an implicit foundation of trust. Her self-proclaimed mission is to help those who have lost belief in themselves by facilitating and encouraging "all persons to believe in and love themselves." She is very good at what she does and she's been doing it for a very long time.

Her office was grand, yet cozy. It didn't reek of institutional fixtures: boring white walls, standard oak furniture, and lousy overhead florescent lighting. No, Anne wouldn't stand for such an uninspiring environment, so she transformed it into a sanc-tuary. There was a window on one end draped with a thick grey curtain. The walls were painted a cool, soothing color. A floor lamp in the corner cast a warming light over her shoulder. Clas-sical music, sometimes barely discernible, wafted through the air like a dream. Freshly cut flowers lent a sweet scent to cover up the standard "school" smell of old paper and stale carpeting. Meticulously maintained plants added to the fresh feeling. She always had a glass pitcher of water, elevating the drinking fountain water to new heights. It was a very intentional environment. Anne created the calm in a boring, standard environment filled with stress, chaos, and competition. It's why I felt safe there.

She continued asking me a series of explorative questions and finally asked if I had ever taken one of those tests that helps you find your best career matches or a Meyers-Briggs assessment to determine my personality traits. What?!? They have a test for that?!? How was it possible that I had made it this far without knowing there was a test out there that tells you what careers you would be happy with and good at? No, I had certainly never taken such a test before and please, when can I sign up? I took both tests that afternoon. When my results came back, they forced me to acknowledge what I already knew inside, but now the cat was out of the bag. I physically had to speak the words. *It became real.* My all-time worst career choice, not a fit at all that topped my list: lawyer. Holy shit! Best career fits in order of best-ness: travel agent, chef, and librarian. What the hell was I doing in law school?

I started to disengage and walk down that oh-so-familiar path. I began being reckless and drinking with abandon. This time, however, I was a little stronger than the last time. I was able to stop, look myself square in the mirror, and say, "No! YOU are NOT going to ruin this too." I booked a plane ticket to Tampa, Florida, to visit my friend Emily. I knew she would help me sort this all out. I was so conflicted. *Do I stay here? Do I leave? If I leave, what will I do?*

The third weekend of October, I flew down to Tampa for four days over the semester's Fall Break from classes. Emily, one of my friends from undergraduate school picked me up from the airport and we went to Geoffrey's apartment to change before heading out on the town that night. Remember Geoffrey? He was that guy I met in St. Petersburg right before I left for New

Zealand.

Geoffrey caught wind of my last-minute travel plans. He hastily broke things off with his girlfriend and called his college buddy in Georgia to cancel their weekend plans. His friend, who was in the Air Force, planned to take Geoffrey backstage and behind-the-scenes at the military air show and perhaps even give him a ride in a fighter jet. Geoffrey had been excited about this opportunity and was looking forward to seeing his old college roommate; however, he dropped it all to gamble on the off chance of seeing me again that weekend.

That night, the three of us went to a dueling piano bar on the waterfront. The next day we had a cookout at Emily's place with a few more friends. Geoffrey enchanted me.

Good grief, he's so goddamn attractive. Why is he even casting his gaze in my direction? If he only knew I was damaged goods.

His gentle blue-grey eyes showed compassion and patience towards me. He looked at me like a treasured goddess, almost like he was in disbelief that I was before him. His smile and words were genuine. I trusted him. My heart fluttered with excitement and I felt like a giggling schoolgirl—then, my head stepped in.

Mary, this is nonsense. Quit playing games and put your head on straight. Now is NOT the time to get wrapped up in some fairytale love fantasy. This is life. REAL life.

We spent the remainder of the weekend together. I didn't really know that much about him, but I had a crush. It was really more than a crush, but all I was willing to admit to myself at the time was that it was a crush.

I was right, visiting Florida would sort things all out, just not the way I anticipated. One problem down, another one to deal with. Deciding whether to continue through law school was the easy problem. After reviewing my finances (and student loan terms), I realized that I could not afford to drop out of law school. If I dropped out of my classes, it was too late to get a refund for tuition, so I would still have to pony up the cash from that semester, which was about $35,000. Oh, and the kicker, it would go into repayment immediately.

I was not confident in my ability to come up with that much money on the fly. As such, I committed myself to completing law school and that meant *committing* my entire self. There could be no half-assing it. I had had my fun. I was trying to leave behind crazy, wild Mary and replace her with this driven, responsible individual who makes practical and rational decisions. No whim. No impulsive decisions from the heart; only carefully thought out decisions from the head. This was not the time or the place to fall back into my old habits, because here, if you didn't make the grades or didn't show up to class: game over. You got kicked out.

Up until fall break, I had been treading water in my classes. Merely treading water spells demise in law school; it means you are staying in the same place while a pack of hungry piranhas circle around you . . . and they *will* eat you without hesitation if you give them the chance. I still had eight weeks or so to pick up my game, get my shit together, and start applying myself. This was good; it forced me to keep my head down and focus with such intensity that I didn't have the opportunity to get sucked into my old habits. I was too tired from school and homework to do anything except sleep.

The second problem, well, it was a real problem. I was over one thousand miles away from a man who stole every thought of every spare moment I had to give, but I was scared and new practical Mary didn't have love on her agenda. New Mary was still hiding. Not in the safety of alcohol or comfort of drug-induced delusions, but in the guise of forced productivity and perfection, which is still not giving credence to my real self. But love, that's a game changer. It forces honesty, especially long distance love where all you have to hang on to are late night conversations, saved emails, and some text messages. There is no physicality, which in this case was a good thing. Sex is another good hiding place that can masquerade as happiness and commitment, and compatibility without actually addressing the real things that create those feelings.

Deep down though, I knew; I knew what it was and what I had to do. It happened just the way my dad always said it would: that love would be unexpected and uncontrollable pure bliss. It was the highest of all highs. I became immediately and insatiably addicted. Here I was, inexplicably intoxicated, unable to fall asleep as I lay in bed in my eleventh floor St. Louis apartment because I was experiencing full on heart-pumping love for the first time and I was about to admit it to myself despite all of the alarms and warning bells sounding from behind the walls I built to protect myself in my head. I closed my eyes tightly and held my breath.

Oh my God. I. Love. Him. Holy Shit! It was the first time I allowed myself the luxury of using those words and truly understanding the gravity of their meaning.

No, not possible! Another voice in my head interrupted. *You can't fall in love with someone that you have met TWICE!* A million voices chimed in together in agreement. *This can't be.* They all said to me. *You don't even know him!*

My eyes were still closed and then I became alarmingly aware that I was still holding my breath. I exhaled abruptly and gasped for air. The voices in my head started to get louder and angrier sounding. *You're not good enough! This is dangerous; be very afraid! You don't deserve love! You had your chance!* The unrelenting taunting continued and then I cracked. I CAN'T TAKE THIS ANY-MORE! I screamed inside.

"NOOOO!" I screamed aloud.

My eyes shot open and I looked around in the darkness almost expecting to see goblins or gremlins scurrying about. I swallowed hard. I knew what I would have done in my past. I would have retreated. I would have shrunk back down into my comfortable corner with my good friends: alcohol and cocaine, but not this time. This could not be ignored. This was *love*, as pure and clean and deep as it comes. I felt it in every part of my body, every muscle, every cell, every fiber of my being.

Something was stirring inside me that had been forced into dormancy, suppressed by years of intentional numbing and hiding from it out of fear. This feeling was part of me now and I knew there would be no shaking off this emotion. There would not be enough alcohol and drugs in the world that could make me numb to this feeling forever, so I had to act. Because if I just let myself shrink back down into the darkness of fear, inaction, and regret, I would be contending with and battling this feeling for the rest of my life in all of the wrong ways.

I smiled and surrendered into the feeling, sensing safety in its warm embrace. Love flooded in and hit me hard and fast. So hard and fast that my inner voices almost didn't have time to ready a fight. I gave myself to permission to say the words out loud.

"I love him," I uttered. My body became awash with warmth. My heart began to speed up with excitement. "I love him. *I love him.* I LOVE HIM!" It was a profound discovery that became real, able to sink in now the words were actually out there, floating around in the universe. I imagine this moment to be similar to the discovery and realization that Thomas Edison had the first time the filament in his light bulb glowed, or when Einstein recognized his theory of relativity. You know, that split second when possibility becomes reality; no longer a "what if", but an "is." When all of the thinking, contemplating, scrutinizing, and speculation make way for absolute certainty.

Suddenly, the whole world needed to know.

I needed to tell everyone.

I needed to tell *him.*

It needed to be in person. And tomorrow wasn't soon enough. I jumped on the next flight to Florida that I could get on. My heart rate didn't slow until I looked into his eyes and saw him. I let him see me, too. And then I said it.

"I love you."

XIV

ADAPT OR DIE

"Yesterday is gone. Tomorrow has not yet come.
We have only today. Let us begin."

MOTHER TERESA

So you might very well be asking yourself why there is a love story in the middle of a book about the entrepreneurial spirit. Well, it's quite simple actually. If you don't know what love is, your eMolecule will be harder to find. When you love someone, truly experience love, you open yourself up. When you open up your heart to love someone, you also open your heart up to possibility. Yes, it can be a risky proposition. You are putting something on the line that you have spent your whole life protecting: yourself. But once you are willing to risk yourself, you begin to realize that it really isn't that scary when you start risking other things, such as money or time. Once you've put the most important thing on the line, you, it no longer seems as risky to look inside, grab your eMolecule, and get started.

Also, love can breed happiness. And I posit that happiness is the platform where fulfillment can begin. It is in this space between happiness and finding fulfillment where your true passions can be found (and finding your passion is the key to fulfillment). And to be clear, happiness feeds your heart; fulfillment feeds your soul. Fulfillment is that greater purpose behind what you do. Happiness is an emotion that passes through you; it is fleeting. Fulfillment doesn't retreat.

But more importantly, it is about identity and change. Getting in touch with your eMolecule is the easy part, but harnessing it will require change and finding your identity. That is when the real work begins. Remember what I said about Darwin at the beginning? Survival is all about adaptation. Opening myself up to experience feelings after so much intentional hiding and self-medicating was scary. No, self-medicating makes it seem like I was helping myself, not harming myself. I was purposefully and methodically tearing myself apart. This new existence with love and feeling was change in a very big way for me.

I was madly in love that was certain. But what to do with that love and how to exist in its presence everyday was challenging. After a year into our relationship, Geoffrey moved to St. Louis, Missouri to close the distance between us to give us a fighting chance to make it as a couple. This turned my world upside down.

This meant I was now accountable to another human being twenty-four hours per day, seven days per week. Disappearing and hiding were no longer options for me. Yes, I had been operating fully in the light for a few years now, but I was still not comfortable being so visible. This new living arrangement exacerbated my discomfort. Since the divorce and coming clean, I had always had a place of my own to retreat to. When I couldn't handle the throes of life, I could escape it by running to my apartment and shutting the door on the world. Leaving all of the madness outside and seeking the comfortable catch of my bed and loving snuggles from my cats. Now, I was surrounded with all of this "we-ness" and I felt as if I had no place to call my own anymore.

I struggled with my identity. It had taken me so long before I was brave enough to stand up on my own. I was just beginning to define *me* and yet, Geoffrey and I were also simultaneously trying to define '*we*'. I feared that I would lose the "me" in the "we" because it had happened before. And if the "me" lost out to the "we" and our relationship failed, then who would I be? How would I define myself? Would I go back to my vices? Would I again become that same thing that I struggled and worked so hard to leave behind? Would I become an addict again? I needed to discover who I was if I wanted to make things work in the relationship, and in order to harness my eMolecule.

I was tenuously perched atop a wire teetering in the breeze trying to hang on and deal with feelings. *Every. Single. Day.* This is the true test of whether you've overcome your addiction, and in my opinion, the shortcoming of many rehabilitation programs. The programs support and assist you as you work on overcoming your addictions, but they don't help you learn how to actually live, how to actually deal with what it feels like to be alive and experience sensation (or at least mine didn't). I mean after all, isn't it sensations and feelings that hook many people onto a path of drug and alcohol abuse? I know that's why I started. I needed to numb my discomfort.

Although I understand that recovery is ongoing (much like growth), rehabilitation programs should continue on until you have your first raw, honest feeling because that's when the shit really hits the fan. Yes, rehab helped me change my relationship with myself and to stop abusing my body, but I achieved that while still circumventing my feelings. Once I overcame my physical chemical dependencies and could "function," I closed myself off immediately. I learned to do exactly what I had done before. I learned how to hide, but just sober. I feared that if I allowed in feeling, then I would open myself up to the possibility of falling into the same traps I set for myself before. I chose to operate by only using my head and leaving my heart out of the equation altogether; it was seemingly safer that way.

Geoffrey changed all of that. My heart was ripped wide open. I didn't want to fall in love. In fact, it was the exact opposite of what I wanted. Yes, love is blissful and beautiful and all of that greatness, but it's the whole cable television package with HBO and Showtime for no extra charge. You get it all: love, peace, humility, anger, jealousy, and fear. There is no a la carte menu where you get to pick and choose what you want to allow yourself to feel. Nope. You get it all. I wanted none of it because feeling emotion fractured my fragile existence. This love knocked me right off that wire and sent me spiraling. In those beginning months, I wanted so badly to run out into the darkness of night and never look back, but I knew disappearing wouldn't help. This was inescapable. My world had been shattered into millions of tiny little pieces and there was no gluing it all back together.

It would never be the same.

I would never be the same.

Yeah, stop and let that sink in for a few minutes. This is what happens when you allow yourself to feel. It's wholly irrevocable. There's no trying it on like a pair of jeans to see if they fit or if you like them. Nope. Once Father Feeling is unshelved, you're buying it, end of story. What are the costs? Not feeling means you don't get to engage in authentic relationships with *anybody* for your *entire life*. Those are high costs that most people, including myself, can't afford, so we have to buy it sooner or later. Life is a precious gift that I tried to squander. To not live it to the fullest would be an insult to our Maker.

Since drugs and alcohol were not an option and running away was out of the question, I did the only thing I could do to survive: I took out all of the rage, hatred, anger, fear, resentment, and love on the one person that brought all of this up to the surface . . . and spent lots and lots of time at the gym and in the kitchen. We also created a "Happiness Calendar." Each night after dinner, we would write down one thing from that day to be happy or thankful about on a huge yellow poster board. This simple task proved difficult for us both on particularly trying days where "ate dinner" or "did a bunch of reading" is all that we could muster as the promising moment from the day. There are also beautiful moments that would otherwise be lost in the jumble of life if we hadn't captured them on the calendar, such as "first snow together" and "laid around in pajamas all day together." These are the moments that make us happy.

When you distill life down one day at time like that, you truly get to see the subtle miracles or small niceties that happen *each and every day* to create your state of happiness. You also begin to notice that these tiny shifts effect big change over time. It is eye opening to put it mildly. This is change. It happens gradually over time as you begin to shift your way of thinking and your point of view, which impacts how you act and respond.

I don't know how Geoffrey handled it all. I knew we had something special, but it wasn't until we were weathering these initial months under the same roof that I began to recognize just how amazing he is. He is a saint. There are not enough words to acknowledge him fully for all that he is and all that he has done for me. Luckily, we don't have to use words with each other when it comes to communicating from the heart. In fact, words tend to get in the way. Just staring into each other's eyes in silence speaks volumes about the love and compassion that we hold for each other in our hearts.

XV

DUDE, LET'S GO FISHING

"You've got to know when to hold 'em, know when to fold 'em,
know when to walk away, know when to run."

KENNY ROGERS,
The Gambler

I am not a quitter. Despite how you may feel about that statement based on the text herein, this is the one thing I want to get straight. Have I made decisions that weren't right? Absolutely. Have I lived those consequences? Yup. Have I had to do damage control to mitigate those consequences or fix what I started? You bet. But I am not a quitter.

Yes, I get afraid and my fear causes indecision, or more truthfully put, total and utter paralysis. But in the end, I always make a decision and that decision is rarely to maintain the status quo. My path through college took me longer than most, but I never gave up, not completely. It was close sometimes. I wanted to succumb or retreat, but in the end I didn't. I am a fighter, an action taker. The path to harnessing my eMolecule, like any path, has temptation. Sometimes temptation completely derails us, other times it is a mere blip on the radar, barely distracting us. And sometimes, it is okay to throw in the towel.

It was a sunny Sunday at the end of July in between my second and third year in law school. I had made the decision to also concurrently study for my Masters in Business Administration while pursuing my Juris Doctorate, as a back-up plan of course, since it was clear that being a practicing attorney wasn't going to necessarily serve me as a solid, happiness-creating career choice. That choice required that I complete twenty-one graduate credits in ten weeks during the summer. (Nine graduate credit hours over the course of a four-month semester is considered full time to give you a frame of reference). To say it was grueling is an understatement. My classmates and comrades will be able to confirm. It was unbearable. I don't know exactly how I did it, I don't need to know how I did it, I just know that I never want to do it again.

I was studying for my Finance exam, but it was not going well. I understood the concepts, but the inner workings of how to properly use a financial calculator were beyond me. "Wait, you mean you don't enter the number, hit the plus sign, and then enter in the other number if you want to add? I'm supposed to enter the number, hit enter, type the other number and then hit the plus sign? Huh?"

Papers were thrashing like leaves during a tornado in fall. Flash cards were thrown into the other room. Frustrated grunts, grumbles and moans soared over the dining room wall into the living room. In terms of throwing a temper tantrum like a three-year-old, I was about four seconds away. Exhaustion had taken hold and my brain stopped answering my requests to recall information. I was at my wit's end. Seconds before the calculator was about to take a one-way plunge off our third-story balcony to its demise, Geoffrey walked into the room.

"Mary! Stop! What is all of this fuss about?"

"I can't do this!" I gestured to the smattering of papers and ripped-up textbook parts strewn about the floor. "I just. CAN'T. DO. THIS!" I yelled emphatically before breaking out into sobs.

"Okay. First, calm down. Because *this*," waving his hands

spastically in front of his face mocking my unjustified tears, "is not helping anything. I think you need to take a break."

"No, I can't. I have to study, otherwise I will fail."

"I thought your professor had some sort of fail-safe policy," he said, referring to a rule my Finance professor had in place during the summer semester for those of us who were crazy enough to take on such a workload. My guess is that the professor had seen this happen before: the total brain meltdown that takes place when there is absolutely no more room for information. As such, he had a lifeline in place. If at any time during the final examination we felt uncomfortable or concerned with our performance, we could turn it in as is and inform him that we wished to take a pass. He would automatically lower our class grade by one letter grade, but that would be the end of it. No failing, no stress, but we had to make the call on whether we wanted to walk away—if walking away was the best we could do.

I nodded my head sheepishly.

"So what is *this* all about? If you decide not to take the exam, what is the worst thing that will happen?"

"I'll get a B." I said heavily as if the world was about to end.

I could tell he was trying not to laugh at me and tell me how ridiculous I was being. Instead, he said gently, "Okay, so if you don't take the final, you'll get a B. If you do take the final, is it possible for you to get lower than a B?"

"Y-Y-Yes." I sniffled. "But I could get an A, too." I finished meekly.

"And what will it take for you to get an A? How long will you have to study? And after all of that time and studying, how likely is it that you are going to get an A? Is it even realistic?"

"I don't know. FOREVER!" as I threw a flashcard at poor Elliot, who was trying to slink by unnoticed. "Not likely. I haven't done well on my quizzes lately. I understand it, but I just can't get it back out right now," I finished, pointing to my head.

"Mary, this is easy. Don't take the final. Just pass and take the

B."

"I can't. I'm not a quitter."

"I know you're not a quitter, but sometimes you just need to know when to quit. Is it really worth all this frustration, stress, anger and time just to try and get an A when you can have a B? That's still a really good grade."

"No, but I can't quit. I have to try."

"You did try. You are trying and now you realize that no matter how much time and effort you put into it, your chances of getting higher than a B are pretty slim. You need to prioritize and figure out how important this grade is to you in the grand scheme of life. Here, let me make you a promise: if you agree to stop this nonsense, pick up your mess, and take the pass, I will take you to the store today and buy you a fishing pole. We'll go fishing in the park. It is beautiful outside and you haven't been outside at all this summer. You need to go outside. You need to take a break. It's okay to walk away sometimes. I know you're not a quitter. You are doing your best and it's amazing. I don't know how you are doing it, but you are. This time, I'm telling you, you need to just throw in the towel. Do we have a deal?"

"B-B-But . . . ," I stammered.

"Call your mom. Tell her you are quitting." He tossed me the phone while it was ringing my mother.

"Hello?," my mom answered.

"I'M A QUITTER!" I burst into tears and snotty snobs immediately upon hearing her voice.

"Hi Mary. You are not a quitter. Tell me what's going on." She said in a concerned, but okay-here-we-go-Mary-what's-this-crisis-all-about sort of way. I love my mother. How she is not completely insane from dealing with my shenanigans and me for all of these years is nothing short of a miracle.

I recapped the events from earlier that day and finished with Geoffrey's fishing offer. My mother, always true to her form, replied, "Mary, have you tried your hardest studying?"

"Uh-huh." I nodded too, just in case she could see me through the telephone.

"Well, as long as you have given it your all and tried your hardest, then you have no choice other than to be happy with the outcome, regardless of the letter grade. Do you have other studying to do for your other classes that you are putting on hold while studying for this test?"

"Yeah." I sniffled, wiping my nose with my sleeve.

"So taking this test might jeopardize your performance in your other classes?" she pressed.

"Yeah, but I . . ." She interjected before I could protest with another excuse.

"There are no 'buts' here, Mary. If what you're telling me is true—and only you will know if it really is—that you tried your hardest and the best you can realistically get is a B and you'll get that letter grade even if you don't take the final, then it seems like you should be happy with a B. What will make you more upset: getting a B in one class or possibly risking your grades in your other courses in order to get one A? Sometimes, Mary, the harder decision is knowing when to walk away. It is easy to just follow the steps we are conditioned to take, but deciding to take a step to the side or walk contra to the flow, that is much more difficult." (Yes, both my mother and Geoffrey speak with profound wisdom).

She continued, "I am so proud of you. I am so proud of what my beautiful, brilliant daughter has accomplished so far in her life. It hasn't been easy and I don't know how you are doing it. I don't know how you can manage your course load. But the most important thing I want you to accomplish is to find happiness, to follow your heart and do what you are meant to do. And for that, unfortunately, sweetheart, there is no test. I wish I could help you. I wish I had the answer and could give it to you, but you have to find it and figure it out for yourself."

I finally stopped sobbing and now was just whimpering. "You mean, you won't be upset at me if I quit?"

"Mary, I will be so proud of you for being brave and following your heart. I already am proud of you."

"So I should quit?"

"I can't make that decision for you, but I will stand behind whatever decision you make. You're the one that has to live with it, not me. I also think Geoffrey is very wise and you are lucky to have him. It's okay to listen to him. He loves you and believes in you, too. He wants the same things I do, for you to be happy and successful. I love you."

She hung up the phone and I just sat there dumbfounded on the floor in the middle of the dining room surrounded by academic debris. *How is this so easy for everyone else to see, except for me?* My sniffles slowed and I started picking up the papers, trying to undo what I had already destroyed. Chester, who had been perched patiently on a chair over my left shoulder for this entire tirade, decided the risk of getting tossed out of the window accidentally had passed, so he courageously hopped down and nuzzled my side. He stared up at me and meowed, as if saying, "You're being completely ridiculous. Don't you see how lucky you are right now? You have worked hard and created opportunities, but you're not taking time to enjoy the fruits of your labor."

He reached down and picked up a yellow highlighter in his mouth and walked a few steps towards the door. When he set it back down, he turned and looked over his shoulder, meowing at me again. I nodded and yelled to Geoffrey, "Fuck it, dude! Let's go fishing!" in an homage to one of my favorite movies, *The Big Lebowski.*

Geoffrey popped off the couch and reached to get his keys. When I got near him, he put his arm around me, "I am so proud of you right now. You are anything but a quitter." He kissed me on the cheek as we headed out the door.

I picked out a black and gold Shakespeare Ugly Stick fishing pole with a Zebco push-button reel. For bait, I picked out a Styrofoam container full of fat, juicy night crawlers and a yellow and orange round bobber. We headed to the park with my new rig, and I sat on a rock the rest of the afternoon contentedly casting away into the stream at my toes. I am not a fancy angler (obviously) and really not much for fishing, but that afternoon it was perfect. I had gotten so caught up in my artificial world, that I disconnected from reality and forgot how beautiful the world is if I just stop long enough to notice. That afternoon, I soaked in sunshine and simplicity, stealing glances at the man who made this possible. I couldn't help but smile and feel happily at ease.

A few days later, it was final exam time. I looked around the classroom as my classmates were anxiously cramming in final equations and nervously squirming in their seats in anticipation. I sat in my seat calmly. I might have even had a hint of a smile on my face. The professor walked in and passed out the exam. Immediately, you could hear papers turning as students were furiously flipping through the pages to preview the content. Erasers were already scuffing out errors. I took a few deep breaths and wrote my name in the top left-hand corner of the cover page. Underneath, I printed in capital letters, "I AM GOING TO TAKE THE PASS" without even leafing through the exam. I stood up from my seat, walked to the desk, and handed in my exam. The professor gawked in surprise. "That's it?" as he flipped through and saw the entire test blank. "You're not even going to try? Don't you want to just look at it?" There were whispers as my classmates looked around at each other, astonished. "Oh my gosh! I can't believe she's just walking out," I heard someone gasp.

"No, professor. I did try. This is the best that I can do." I held strong in my steadfast statement regarding my efforts.

"In all my years of teaching since I instated this policy, I have never had anyone not even try to take the exam. Usually, students will at least attempt at few problems before deciding to quit . . ." He trailed off.

"Well, sir. It is my understanding of the stated policy that attempting or completing a portion of the exam before exercising the pass option is not a prerequisite. Moreover, as I said before, I did try. I gave this class my all and after examining the opportunity costs and investment required to achieve a result above that of the pass option, I would experience a negative ROI (return on investment). As such, I choose to exercise the pass option."

"Uh, umm, you are correct. But what are you going to do now?"

"Well, it's a beautiful day outside. I think I'm going to go fishing." I smiled and turned on my heels toward the door.

Something crazy happened that day, too: nothing. Absolutely nothing. The world did not come crashing down around me. I didn't explode. There was no Armageddon or Apocalypse. You know, all of the "reasonable" consequences that you would expect from my end-of-the-world rant days earlier. Nope. The worst that could have happened from that decision did in fact happen, and I received a B in that class. Turns out, that's not the end of the world either, as I had predicted.

And no one thought any less of me except for my professor, perhaps. In fact, quite the opposite happened. Upon returning to classes the next day, my fellow classmates were coming up to me commenting on the size of my "balls." "Man, I wish I had the balls just to write my name on the test and turn it in without looking at the problems. I sat there for two and a half hours before I took the pass option. I can't believe I wasted all of that time." Or, "Holy shit, Mary! That was awesome! Did you see the look on the professor's face? I can't believe you did that!" I sort of became a little bit of viral school lore as students passed the story along to one another. Of course, there was the inevitable group that judged me negatively: "I can't believe you just quit like that. Slacker." To them, I can now say, "Yeah, but I still graduated with honors just like you and guess what? Nobody gives a damn about that and certainly not about the fact that I got a B in my Finance class." That would be, if I cared to waste my breath on responding at all.

Now I know this entire story is ridiculous and some of you are reading disgustedly, saying to yourself, "Seriously? You got this worked up over a freakin' B?" Yes. Yes I did, at that moment, it was important to me and it was a breaking point. That summer, in addition to my classes, I was also working part time for a professor at the school of law. I had way overcommitted myself because I was afraid to say no to opportunities. I was operating a balancing act on a thin wire and the whole grade thing just set me off, but I don't want to get hung up on the grade, because that's not the part that matters. What matters is that I learned that it is okay to say "no" or to quit if something is truly not in your best interest AND this is much harder to do than saying "yes."

Why is it harder to say no? Because it requires a lot of gutsy stuff. It means that you are putting *yourself* above the needs, wants, desires, or expectations of someone else *and* you are secure enough in that decision to face judgment, both internally from yourself and from others with possible confrontation or guilt. It means (a) you respect that you are valuable and have self-worth, (b) you recognize that saying no or quitting serves your interests better than continuing, (c) you trust your own voice to follow your heart or your gut, and (d) you follow through and stand your ground to not fall prey to guilt. Now that takes courage and bravery, which is why it is so much easier to "go with the flow" and say "yes." You can skip over all of the internal exploration and rest easy that you're still saving face and maintaining expectations. No one will question you. Probably because they are also afraid to confront you even more than you are afraid to confront yourself.

I struggled with saying "No" and still struggle with this today. I could give you a thousand examples where I said "yes" and really wanted to say "no," but a lot fewer examples of where I chose *me* instead, and didn't put myself on the backburner or sacrifice myself in exchange for something that someone else needed from me. I chose this example. Am I a quitter? Nope, but it certainly may look like it to the outside world. That's the other piece to saying no. It's very personal because it is such an internal, personal process. To some, my decision to not take the exam may have seemed like a no-brainer. Yet to others, I might come off as a quitter or slacker. No courage needed to make that decision, right? Clearly, not. To me, it was a very difficult decision that I struggled with.

Why is it so difficult to say this tiny little word "No"? Because it is seemingly difficult to respect yourself and truly embrace your value. We tend to focus on our pitfalls, not our strengths. It takes practice to assess the positive before noticing the negative. Under certain circumstances it is easier than others. But saying "no" forces us to respect and trust ourselves. It forces us to acknowledge our own wants and needs, even if just for a tiny moment before committing to "no." It forces us to overcome self-doubt.

XVI

ON THE ROAD TO DESTINY, DON'T EAT THE SALAD

"If opportunity doesn't knock, build a door."

MILTON BERLE

Yes, the girl who decided to go to law school to start her own business and not have to pay an attorney now had wild notions of becoming a super-successful practicing attorney. I guess you could say that I went to law school to become an anti-attorney, the complete opposite of a practicing attorney. I wanted to learn some specific skills and keep them all to myself. However, I, like my classmates, caught barrister fever and it infected me like a virus that no antibiotic could cure. Well, yes, the I'm-gonna-be-a-lawyer-plague was going around, but I was also just plain tired of dealing with the strange looks of confusion when I explained to people the real reasons why I came to law school. At some point between my first and second year of law school, my fake answer, "I want to go into securities litigation, possibly the enforcement side," became the truth in my mind, probably because I had used it so many times I just plum forgot the real reasons why I started law school. This fake answer also helped me fit in with my peers and as we have all experienced, it can be much easier to go with the flow than try to swim against it. So I succumbed to the path of least resistance almost unknowingly.

This "new truth" was somewhat problematic because nothing in my past work history or educational background really pointed to the desire that I now shared to become a securities litigator. As such, scoring summer internships or clerkships proved difficult on the basis of a resume alone. I decided to leverage my winning personality (feel free to snicker here) and meet people in the industry who would, at least in my new securities litigation fantasy world, absolutely be impressed by my professional demeanor that they would hire me on the spot, no resume needed. Did it work? The short answer surprisingly is yes.

In order to make it happen, I had to swallow my pride and take a huge judgment prevention pill because I had to surrender myself to one of the top five worst events ever conjured up: a bar association ladies' luncheon. I am allowed to say this because first, I am a woman, and second, I am an attorney, and I do believe that we are given permission to prod at the social, ethnic, and gender classifications that we, ourselves, belong to. Now, it's not that I hate ladies or lunch, but ladies luncheons elicit the same feelings of nausea and dread that I get when I receive an invitation to a baby shower or wedding shower, except at a luncheon there is no cake and usually nothing to celebrate, which are the only two real high points at a shower. The luncheon does have the bonus of not having any ridiculous but obligatory little games that no one really wants to play, and there are no requirements to "oooo" and "ahhhh" like it's the Fourth of July as little Betty Bride opens up another fondue pot or electric wok. So in this regard, I salute men for not creating these silly events for one another and I applaud women who make these events co-ed so that our other halves are forced to suffer through our same fate.

Luncheons of any variety tend to suck, but those solely for women are just worse than those where both genders are represented. First, at a ladies luncheon, everyone drinks water with lemon. There is the occasional iced tea with Splenda or artificial sweetener of choice and a few speckled orders for diet-anything soda. Second, there seems to be a wide misconception that women are like rabbits and really like to eat salad.

Now, I'll admit, I do like salad, but not salad of the luncheon variety which always seems to consist of wilted Sysco Spring Mix, you know, the one with baby spinach, baby lettuces, and a few pieces of chopped-up radicchio, topped with packaged croutons and a very scant amount of sliced grape tomatoes, cucumber, and possibly some slivers of roasted red pepper, if you're lucky. There are always two dressing options: low-fat ranch (eeeeewwwwe) and this thick, unworldly pink dressing that is possibly raspberry, but could also indistinguishably be strawberry vinaigrette (it is very hard to tell because the dressing tastes nothing like either fruit) with a sprinkle of poppy seeds so that every woman who selects the thick pink goop will spend the rest of the lunch worried about all of the little black specks of poppy seeds that are stuck in her teeth.

If it is a higher-end luncheon, like the bar association function that I attended, you of course are also served a wedge of quiche because for some odd reason unbeknownst to me, at least, quiche seems like it's healthy even though it's really just eggs, cream, and cheese baked in a pastry crust made with copious amounts of butter, lard or shortening (maybe all three, who knows?). Mark my words, ladies; if I ever host a luncheon, I will serve bacon cheeseburgers, so fear not.

Aside from the food, conversation at luncheons is so trivial and contrived. There are the formal introductions, followed by the brief description of current position and goals, and the obligatory nod to family and kids, if applicable. No one walks in and says, "Hi. My name is Mary. I'm here to meet the speaker to see if she will give me a job. If she won't, perhaps I will wow one of you at my table and you will want to bring me on board. If not, then this is a complete waste of time. So, why are you here (because we all know it's not for the salad)?" Instead, we all dance around the real reasons that forced us into this situation in the first place and fake smile at one another. I was at this particular luncheon to do just that or at least perform some recon on the major players in securities litigation in my fair city. I, however, wasn't able to fake smile and pretend like I was eating the best salad in the world for the entire length of the luncheon, so about one-third of the way through the luncheon I let my intentions be known to the ladies that I was dining with.

The result: I met the speaker. She had a boring presentation, but is a very engaging individual and she provided me with some excellent tips. I also "wowed" one of the women at my table with my frankness who suggested that I reach out to a few individuals in her network. And this is the beginning of the real point of this soliloquy: I reached out to the former Securities Commissioner for the great state of Missouri. (I would like to interject that when I went to a presentation by the Secretary General of the United Nations, Bahn Ki Moon, he pronounced Missouri as 'misery,' which gave everyone in the audience quite a chuckle). We met for lunch and he gave me all sorts of tips on how to get into the industry.

I myself have been on the other end of these arrangements, where students are looking at me to give them their dream job or at least some hot leads on how to get there, but I most certainly disappoint them when I instead ask them to explain why this is their chosen career path and delve into questions of happiness and self-exploration, which always makes me feel a little bad because we both know they are really there to see if I will hire them so they can stop going on all these lunch dates with people three times their age where they have to pretend to give a shit about what the other person is saying.

A few months passed and the former Missouri Securities Commissioner and I kept in touch through email. I found myself no further down the road to becoming the next big thing at the Securities and Exchange Commission, and he had just started his own law practice. Frustrated and fed up, I invited myself to his new office under the pretense of a tour and a quick "catch up," but I was really there to get a job and wouldn't walk away with anything less. I wore my best (and favorite) suit dress: a brown tweed number with matching belt at the empire waist. Not flashy, just pulled together and professional.

The office suite was in the corner of a large high-rise building near an affluent part of town. There was a small lobby with a front desk where a polite receptionist nearly covered in tattoos from head to toe greeted new clients and postal workers. There was a wall behind the front desk with another desk area where the office manager sat. She, too, was very friendly and polite. I learned that we had the same birthday, so as birthday sisters, we were destined to become good friends. Outside of the office manager's work area, the hallway was lined with built-in filing drawers that ended when the hallway took a sharp ninety-degree turn past the three windowed offices for the firm's attorneys. The hallway dead-ended into the corner office where the former Securities Commissioner, the firm's Managing Partner, set up shop.

His office was large, but awkwardly shaped so that the furniture couldn't be arranged in a practical fashion. His giant u-shaped desk cut off the entrance and a black leather sofa protruded across the other side of the office, emphasizing the strange triangular-ish shape of the room. Behind the sofa sat the mandatory ficus tree that seems to be in all office spaces, but thankfully there were no pretentious bookshelves full of matching leather-bound law books or tufted leather chairs. I sighed in relief as I read the plaque under a neon yellow and turquoise Mahi-Mahi replica that hung on the wall. I thanked the tattooed receptionist for showing me back to the Managing Partner's office and smiled as I shook his hand. I congratulated him on his new office and commented on the neutral, mostly unpretentious décor. We made some brief small talk before I cut to the chase— no bull shit, no dancing around the real reason—we both already knew why I was here anyway.

"So, Managing Partner, thank you for inviting me to see your new office. It's fantastic." I complimented him one more time. "I imagine that you'll be getting pretty busy and will need some additional help around here very soon. As you already know, I am interested in getting into securities litigation myself, so I could certainly learn a lot from someone of your experience and caliber." I flashed another smile as he was gearing up for rebuttal. "I can be your law clerk. Your time is certainly better spent communicating with clients and practicing your craft. I can handle the research for you to free up your valuable time to do what you do best. I am merely looking for experience with no long-term commitment to hire me full time upon graduation, because after all I want to head into the government sector, not private practice."

"I don't really have a need for a law clerk right now." He stated flatly.

"You most certainly do. Think about the number of hours you spend researching legal issues to include in motion briefs. I can research those issues for you and put it all in a concisely drafted memoranda. You'll spend less time performing menial research and more time planning and executing litigation strategy."

"Hmmmmm . . . but I can't pay you. I'm operating on a tight budget since we just opened," he firmly objected.

"You don't have to pay me. Remember, I'm here to get experience to add to my resume and possibly a professional reference from you. We can operate as though this is an unpaid internship."

"Yeah, but I don't have any more desk space or office space for you."

"Oh, not a problem! I believe I saw a folding table and chair in between the copy machine and the microwave in the break room. I have a laptop, so I'm mobile and can work anywhere. It's no bother. Everyone has to start somewhere." Another smile.

"I don't think I . . ."

"It's a win-win," I interjected before he could continue. "You need my help. I need the experience. We can do a trial run. If you don't like my skills or find there is no work for me to do, no problem, I'll leave. All I ask for in return is a letter of recommendation upon my departure."

"Yeah, but . . ."

"Thank you, Managing Partner, for this opportunity. I will do my best. I look forward to working with you and can't wait to get started."

"Um, okay, uh, great. I guess I will see you on Monday morning at 9 A.M.?" He seemed confused as to what had just taken place.

"Sounds perfect. Enjoy the rest of the day and have a great weekend!" I popped out of his office before he could change his mind.

Coercion? Perhaps. Manipulative? Maybe. But I was honest about my intentions and didn't waste his time. On the same token, I didn't just sit back and wait for something to happen. I made it happen. *I took action.*

Shaping your destiny is exactly that: taking action. Yes, your eMolecule will help light your fire, but what you do with that fire will determine your success. The way I see it, there are only two options: sitting back and waiting for perfect opportunities to happen to you, which means you will probably be waiting for a long time or you can go out there and act to create your own opportunities. Neither option is right nor wrong, you can certainly choose either one; they will both shape your destiny, but only one will lead you down a path to your eMolecule.

XVII

TRUST THE UNIVERSE

"You can't blame anyone else, . . . , no one but yourself. You have to make your own choices and live every agonizing day with the consequences of those choices."

MAX BROOKS

My mother always told me that God will never give you more than you can handle. Two things I have come to realize about my mother: she actually is always right and, no, I never seem to give her the credit. Anyway, right now, I am super angry at God. He knew the delicate line that I was balancing on and then he throws all of this crap at me. So, not cool, God. We're not friends right now, and I'm not talking to you for a while.

Geoffrey and I were newlyweds. I was a fresh graduate with two advanced degrees. He'd just finished his Master's programs. Life finally seemed to show hope and promise. If ever there are tangible moments of achievements, it is at a graduation. You can physically hold that real piece of paper that stands for hard work, sacrifice, learning, and possibility. You can finally rejoice, "YES! I made it to the finish line!" but the wind gets knocked out of your sails before you even start moving because you realize that you don't know what comes next. *I have all of this hope, motivation, and knowledge. I am ready to take on the world, but where do I start?* We'd moved back to our happy place: Florida. Things were going to be okay. We felt so much promise and potential. So why was God doing this to me? To us?

The job opportunity that made us feel secure in moving to Florida didn't pan out the way we had hoped or planned, and we were relying on me to be the breadwinner, while Geoff got his business off the ground or found a job. The economy was total shit. There were zero jobs to be had for professionals in our new town. The only jobs available: retail clerks, golf pros, and hospitality staff to serve the booming tourism season here. Did I mention that I was also studying for the bar exam? We were between the proverbial rock and a hard place. We were flat broke. We had sold most of our possessions to move to Florida and our "nest egg," as tiny as it was, was used to cover the security deposit, first month's rent, and last month's rent on the condo we'd leased.

We tried to purchase a condo, but were unable to secure financing despite our ability to put twenty percent down because we couldn't show proof of income in Florida. Geoffrey was the primary source of income in Missouri, but he obviously didn't have that job anymore, and we were unable to posit how much my earnings would be. Loan underwriting had just been severely restricted due to the recent financial crisis where pillars of the banking industry were imploding on themselves. Thus, our only viable option was to blow our entire savings on a rental.

I was essentially useless from an income and mortgage lending standpoint while studying for the bar exam. During this time, I worked remotely for the same law firm that I had finagled a job with a few years prior in St. Louis. It didn't sit well with Managing Partner that he wasn't paying me, so a few months into our arrangement he started paying me a monthly salary of $500. In St. Louis, the amount wasn't critical to our bottom line because of Geoffrey's salary, but now those $500 monthly paychecks were absolutely critical to our bottom line and were definitely not covering our monthly living expenses. Sometimes, I would get a "bonus" and my check would be for $1500.

I had several discussions with Managing Partner about our financial situation, but my pleas seemed to fall on deaf ears. Either Managing Partner and the firm were not in the financial position to do anything to assist us, or Managing Partner was satisfied and able to sleep soundly with the knowledge that he was paying a full time employee significantly below the minimum wage. Could I have technically pushed for the statutory minimum? Yes, I suppose I could have, but this is a bit like biting the hand that feeds you. You just don't do it, especially if that is the only hand that is feeding you. I was also still battling internally with my eMolecule and it wasn't quite clear yet, who would win the fight.

The initial career plan that moved us to Florida, had been that I would open up a branch office for the law firm in Naples upon passing the bar exam to service the existing clients that the firm had in Florida and help grow the firm's business in the state. This seemed like a good plan, aside from some serious flaws. Well, as this D-day of sorts drew nearer, it became evident to me that it wasn't going to work. I respect where Managing Partner was coming from, but I am not certain that he actually respected where I was coming from.

Could I open and lead the firm? Yes, absolutely. I had no doubt about my ability to perform. But then there was the question of money. One doesn't just get a law firm opened up at no cost, but then again I didn't have any money and Managing Partner had failed to firm up any clear delineation of costs, budgets, and how much money he expected me to pony up. It took until after we had completely relocated, and I had spent several thousand dollars on bar prep classes and exam registration fees for him to give me my "buy in" amount.

In retrospect, this happened all backwards. But you know the old saying, "Fool me once, shame on you. Fool me twice, shame on me." I pretended to be too naïve and seemed too trusting of Managing Partner's words because he was telling me what I wanted to hear. I was also too scared to listen to the warning bells going off in my head, screaming about failed due diligence and blatant violations of common sense. I justified my ignorance with more fear: the fear that if I listened to myself, to what I knew in my heart was right, then Geoffrey and I wouldn't get to move to Florida, that I would talk myself out of moving altogether—and that meant breaking my promise to Geoffrey.

When I told Managing Partner that I couldn't come up with the buy-in money he requested, it only angered him. Managing Partner felt that I had led him on and that I was unrealistic to think that the firm would cover the full cost to open the Florida office. Naturally, I saw it from the exact viewpoint that it was completely unrealistic for him to think I could come up with any real sum of money to "invest" in the firm especially since I had only been making $500 a month for the last two and a half years. He was essentially asking me to return every penny he'd ever paid me, and there would be no guaranteed monthly income.

Completely unheard of? Not necessarily, but also it wasn't exactly setting me (or the firm's Florida office) up for success. When I pleaded my case before him, he didn't listen. I felt as if he had turned his back on me and flagrantly disregarded the toil and hard work of the previous few years. When I asked him for help—as a peer and a friend—he turned me away. Let's not even go down the path of trying to ask him for a monthly income so we could afford to live. Suffice it to say, he barked that maybe Geoff should get a job. Thanks a lot Captain Obvious, we're relentlessly trying on that front.

I know that I let Managing Partner down, but he let me down too. Perhaps this was a relationship destined for failure. Who knows? We both had a lot invested in the decision to create a Florida office, but he only seemed to acknowledge his risk. Mine didn't seem to matter to him. This cut deep because, despite our differences, we were tight-knit, like family. The entire office was.

I looked up to him, as did the other attorneys under his wing. He was our fearless leader, teaching us the art of wordsmithing and litigation, so we all could step into greatness as attorneys. I tried my hardest to appease him with my work and make him proud. He was tough. He was explosive. He would go on profanity-clad rampages through the office when something didn't go his way. Fortunately, I rarely was the object of such rage, but it made everyone feel like they had to tiptoe around on eggshells. He's Irish. I guess maybe that's one explanation, though doubtful.

Regardless of his methods, I learned so much. He improved and honed my skills to a level close to perfection. The worst part is I don't think I ever really thanked him for taking a chance on me. I guess he didn't thank me either. When I realized we were doomed for failure, I pulled the plug. I aborted the mission. Sometimes, you have to know when to throw in the towel, right? Needless to say, it went pretty much as planned, which means it didn't go well. In true, yet fully anticipated fashion shortly after I delivered the fatal blow, I received the most scathing, hurtful email from Managing Partner that you could ever imagine. It covered all of the bases: profanity, sexism, innuendo, and unprofessionalism. It was not the way I wanted it to end, but I guess it really was the only way it was ever going to end with him. Two days later, I received my bar exam results. I failed. Awesome.

There it is for the entire world to see: *I failed.* There are only a handful of people that knew that up until now. Well, that cat's out of the bag now. *Breathe, Mary. It was bound to be found out sooner or later.*

This was supposed to be my pinnacle moment. The apex where I proved to myself and to the world that *I am a do-er.* This is not the part of the story where I fail. My head, as usual, started to chime in.

This is supposed to by my big moment of TRIUMPH! WHY?!? Why are you letting this happen to me, God? Haven't I been through enough? Haven't I proven myself to you? When do I get to lie down in paradise? When is it my turn?

I stared at the computer screen. Next to my bar exam registrant number in big red capital letters, there it was: **F-A-I-L.** I went numb. I didn't cry. I couldn't feel. I was in shock. My body refused to move. My voices came back. They taunted me.

What made their taunting so unbearable was that they were right. I knew I'd failed long before I saw the results publicly plastered on the screen before me. I walked out of that huge room at the convention center leaving behind 10,000 other attorney hopefuls, knowing that I would not go from hopeful to actual. I'd hoped that the bar exam results wouldn't manifest themselves like this, but deep down I knew that I had failed.

You might be saying to yourself right now, "Well, you tried Mary. You did the best you could. Don't be upset or angry at yourself." If you are, I have you fooled. The real truth is, I didn't try. Yes, I studied and had done some of exercises, but *I didn't really do them.* I just merely went through the motions. I tried to justify to myself that I had tried. I lied to those around me and told them that I had tried. They believed me, but I was a *liar.* I deceived them, but I couldn't deceive myself and it haunted me.

By now, you know that my mom is a very wise person. Growing up, she impressed upon us sisters that although performance and grades are important, they are not nearly as important as effort. She would always be proud of us no matter the results, as long as we truthfully put our best efforts forward. This "truth" comes with a very big and very important caveat. She taught us that we would be able to lie to others and tell them we really, really tried, but we would have to live with the guilt that not only had we received the consequences we deserved from our actions, but also that we had just lied about it. We would be the only ones that could carry that burden; no one else simply would be able to. So, it would be up to us whether we could live with that burden or not.

And, like I've also said, my mom is always right. I got exactly the results I deserved, and then I lied about it. Nope. It turns out that I cannot live with that kind of knowledge and carry around all that guilt either. She certainly knew that, too, but nevertheless she let us choose our own fates. She knew that we would never actually learn the lesson, except through self-discovery.

More importantly, my mother had faith that eventually, we would choose correctly. Job well done, Mom. You are an amazing parent. That guilt is like a carnivorous spore that just eats at you day in and day out, but will never actually kill you; it will just make you miserable—that my friends, is shame. We don't like to share our shame and we keep it hidden from others, but the more we hide it, the more it eats at us. It makes us vulnerable. It makes us feel worthless. I have spent a lot of time with shame. I have allowed myself to be consumed by it, so that my actions are borne out of hiding and shame instead of the real me. It is absolutely exhausting carrying shame around every day.

So here I am, curled up in a self-built fortress of bed pillows surrounding me in the corner of my bedroom, heaving heavy sobs full of shame. I had no one to blame but myself for this failure. I knew my husband was counting on me to come through, at least once, especially *this time*.

"Why am I self-sabotaging my success? What am I afraid of? What's wrong with me? Why is it that I let myself do this to myself? If I can't clean up my act for me, do it for Geoffrey. He has done nothing but love you unconditionally and have faith in you. Why must I continually test his faith in me?"

This is what self-inflicted failure feels like. But there's hope. I didn't seek solace in the liquor cabinet, a sketchy alley, or do a transaction in a Wal-Mart parking lot. No way. I just sat there in the corner forcing myself to sit in the squalor I had created. Oh God, how I wanted to numb myself. The urges were unbearable. I thought that I might go insane if I had to sit there a moment longer.

"This is what torture feels like. I bet this is what hell feels like: an urge you can never fulfill, a thirst that is unquenchable, a desire that is insatiable. Yup. This is definitely my preview of hell."

I didn't want to feel anything and I most certainly did not

want to feel this. I closed my eyes, thinking back to that night when I was lying on the black Pontiac in Georgia. Part of me yearned to go back there, to make the choice I didn't make.

"Well Mary, you had your chance to make that choice, to go down that road, but you didn't. You are here now. Be here. Feel this. You made yourself feel this way. You chose, now live with the consequences. You don't get to numb the pain like that anymore. You chose, and that wasn't your choice."

"But I don't want to be here."

"But you are. If you don't want to be here, what are you going to do about it?"

"I can't . . . do . . . anything . . . I . . . don't . . . know . . . what . . . to . . . do . . ." I whined back at myself.

"Yes, yes you do, but only you can do it. No one else will be able to take that test for you."

"I can't."

"Then don't. No one is making you. But then you have to sit here and feel this forever. If you don't, then your shame will never go away and you will still be in this place of limbo. You have come so far. If you weren't going to finish, then why did you even bother starting? Don't you remember why you're here? The reasons you went to law school; what you learned? How will you help people if you can't help yourself?"

I don't know about you, but when someone challenges me (even if that challenge comes from within) and purports that I can't do something, I get all fired up.

"Oh yeah?!? You don't get to tell me what to do! I am the boss of me! You didn't think I would be able to stay clean after this one, huh? Well, I did. So THERE! You don't think I can finish what I started? Well guess what? I'm NOT A QUITTER!!! Watch me!" I yelled back at myself.

And here is the part where I just sit in my pillow fortress because I don't know what else to do. Decision to not let fear get the best of me. Check. Now what? What I really wanted to do was just stay in my pillow fortress and sleep. I wanted to sleep and then, like some *Rip Van Winkle* story, wake up and this would all just be resolved and gone.

Oh, I almost forgot to share this juicy tidbit. My law classmates and peers across the nation that graduated when I did were named by the American Bar Association as the "Lost Generation." Great. Now I am officially classified as lost and there are statistics showing how much less money we will make in our lifetimes, how much less likely we are to get hired as lawyers when the legal industry begins hiring again, and how much less statistical chances at "success" we have, however that is defined by the ABA. That is exactly the news I was hoping for as I still smarted from slap of failing the bar exam. Fuck this. This is NOT how this is supposed to turn out! Oh, how I wanted to blame the world for all of this!

For starters, we needed money. Here we were, two people with five college degrees and we were jobless and broke. We did what we were supposed to, right? Aren't there all sorts of studies and government propaganda out there that seem to promise a better life if you invest in your education? "Go To College! Be Successful! Make More Money!" seemed to be the chant of our day, as if to say, "If you don't go to college then you'll be miserable and broke." We, college graduates, were forced to go on welfare just so we could eat. A half-million dollars in education between us and we were on food stamps.

Now all political controversy aside, welfare is supposed to be a safety net for people who have fallen and need help getting back up. And man, did we need help. I have nothing against welfare programs that help people get on their feet, but it is a humbling experience to swallow your pride and your ego to ask for help in the most public of ways. I had officially brought shame of a new degree into our house. I was embarrassed that I could not provide for my family. I blamed myself for creating this situation and bringing Geoffrey into my mess. I worried that we had a negative stigma now. We really didn't. No one knew. It's not something that we openly shared. However, we had made a few friends in our neighborhood and as we got closer, one of my friends was telling me about the money troubles she was having. I opened up and told her about our financial woes; I told her we were on welfare. Needless to say, these "friends" began to disassociate with us.

Perhaps you can relate or perhaps you are creating your own image in your mind of the type of people that utilize welfare. If you want to know what someone who has been on welfare looks like, then look into my face. Look at me, look at my husband and then pass your judgments. Just keep it dignified. We are proud. We are still people. We needed help. We needed you. So thank you taxpayers for helping us when we needed it most. We are here for you, too, when you need us.

This unsavory stigma that had descended onto our house was enough for me to break down the walls of my pillow fortress and take me from just decision into actual action. I never wanted to feel ashamed like this again. I never wanted to see my husband ashamed of our situation or me. Lost Generation or not, I was going to move forward. I had to. *I am not another statistic to paint a picture of doom and gloom with! I am a human being. Your statistics hurt me. They don't describe me. You don't get to call shots on my future. I get to do that. Not you!*

It became clear what I had to do. I had to finish what I had started. I was relentless this time. I attacked the bar exam material. I studied harder and longer than I ever have, and, quite frankly, ever want to again. When I sold my bar exam study material, the books alone, without the 5,000+ flashcards I made or binders full of notes, weighed 28 pounds. I won't speculate exactly on length. This time, when I passed through those doors into the Tampa Convention Center, I knew that I had honestly tried as hard as I could. If I failed, then it was out of my hands and I would find a different opportunity or solution. I would not be taking the bar again.

That didn't happen. I passed. I nailed it. I was a fully licensed (jobless) attorney. I was and am so proud of myself for not losing it, when losing it was so close. I could have easily slid down that slippery slope, but I didn't. I was still standing and I stood tall.

During this time in our lives, despite the sleepless nights worrying about how rent was going to get paid, we were happy. We were together. We were healthy. When you're in the thick of it, it sucks. Looking back is so much easier. But no matter how bad it was the universe provided what we needed. Yes, sometimes it came down to the eleventh hour, but we never paid our rent late. We did whatever it took to hold steadfast to our responsibilities. Our instinctual eMolecules kicked in. We sold off more of our possessions. We picked items up out of the trash, cleaned them up, and sold them on Craigslist. Somehow, something would always come through at the last minute: a new client for Geoffrey's business or a great garbage find would be the final push to being able to pay our bills.

We even were afforded a special anniversary retreat. Geoffrey entered a YouTube contest to win a trip to Key West by creating a viral video for a transportation company. He won. We celebrated our very first wedding anniversary in Key West during a hurricane. It was absolutely miserable outside, but we were starry-eyed the entire time. There is nothing quite like trudging down Duval Street waist-deep in filthy water, shivering. At least it was memorable. We joke that if it had been the storybook-perfect celebration, it wouldn't have been nearly as memorable. It always seems that we find our deepest happiest and appreciate our love the greatest in life's most imperfect moments.

Years later, when I met my mentor for the first time, he told me the exact same things that my mother had told me: "You will be able to handle whatever life throws at you." And although I had heard it a zillion times before, hearing it from a complete stranger who knew nothing about me seemed to force me to actually listen, to actually trust myself. He casually asked me about my path.

"So, Mary, what is it that you do?"

"Well, actually, I'm in the process of redefining that."

"So what is it that you do?"

"Well, I'm hoping to help inspire entrepreneurs. I'm trying to put together an educational platform. I'm trying to write a book that will be inspirational. I don't know. I guess I'm just trying stuff."

"Will your book help people?"

"I hope so."

"If it will help people, why isn't it finished?"

"Well, er, umm."

"Are you worried about money?"

"Yes."

"What if I told you I could give you financial freedom? Would you say yes?"

"Ummmm, yes, of course," I stammered.

"Here," he said, tossing me a box of business cards. I caught the cards. "Now throw it back to me."

I tossed the box back at him and he threw it right back at me. I reacted by catching the box again, but was very perplexed. "Throw it back to me again," he instructed.

I did, and he immediately passed it right back to me. I began to get a little irritated. *What the hell are we doing? This isn't financial freedom.*

"There. I just gave you financial freedom," he stated.

Still confused, I just shot him a puzzled look in response.

"You wanted financial freedom and I just gave it to you. What did you do when I threw the box at you?"

"I caught it."

"Yes, yes you did. And did you feel stressed about it? No. You just caught it. It was a reflex. *You caught it each time.* You see, Mary, you will never be thrown anything you can't handle. It may not always seem as simple as catching a box, but it actually is just that simple. So, I'll ask you again. Will your book help people?"

"I'm hoping it will."

"Stop thinking! You're being wishy-washy. Will your book help people?"

"Yes." I started to cry. His stare was penetrating, inescapable. I tried to hide, but he wouldn't let me. I didn't even know this guy and yet I was telling him my deepest darkest, most protected things about me. It scared the shit out of me.

"Then why isn't it finished? If it will help people, why are you depriving people who need your help from getting it?" He continued, "Why do you want to help people?"

"Because I can. Because it is fulfilling. Because it is what I was meant to do."

"Then do it. Every day you are not helping people is another day you deprive someone from getting help. You are valuable. You are a warrior. You are a leader. Now go. People need you."

I still get goose bumps and butterflies when I think about those few moments. My eyes began to well with tears from this seemingly chance encounter because this stranger had authentic confidence and faith in me. He knew what my mother always knew about me: I am courageous. I am strong. I will help free people, just like I was able to free myself. This time, it really hit home. It's amazing how far I'd come, yet how close I still am to where I started.

Why am I telling you this? Because years later, I still need to be reminded of this. Because we are all courageous and strong, you will always be able to handle what life throws at you. Yes, you may need help from time to time, but you can do it. Remember, you are brave, too. The moral of the story is that you are strong enough to step up to the plate, to tackle the challenge even if it doesn't feel like it. Have faith in the universe. Have faith in yourself. I do.

In fact, when things are easy, they often go unnoticed. It is the imperfections and the hard times that we look back on and smile about. Because it is in these times that we realize what we are made of. We get an opportunity to really assess needs versus wants. We learn that no matter how bad it gets, there is still happiness to be found there. It may take on a different shape or activity. Maybe you find yourself foregoing orchestra performances in favor of free outdoor concerts in the park, but the point is, you still are able to not only muster through it, but you are still able to find simple pleasures to bring happiness to this place. Without these hard times, we wouldn't be able to appreciate how sweet the good times really are.

Remember this. This is key to harnessing your eMolecule.

XVIII

$49 FRIEND: PRICELESS

*"The camera is an instrument that teaches people
how to see without a camera."*

DOROTHEA LANGE

I am so grateful for all of the extraordinary individuals I have met along the way. You know the ones I am talking about, the ones that never cease to amaze. They are the ones that have the ability to see *you*. It's like they have X-ray vision and peer through all the walls and blankets and coats that you wear to protect your most intimate, vulnerable thoughts, feelings, and parts. And then, after glimpsing at your true self, it's like they don't even see all the stuff you keep in there that you label as bad; they just see your shining parts. They see you for all that you are. They see greatness.

Well, while I was dealing with my emotions of failure and shame from not passing the bar exam, I met one of these extraordinary people. We met as the result from a simple $49 Groupon purchase for a photography session so I could have some professional, lawyerly photographs taken. The Groupon was purchased before I failed the bar exam and before I was jobless. I remember that I almost didn't go because I was so ashamed of myself.

I feared that the photographer would take one look at me and know my secrets: addiction, failed bar exam attempt, and that I was jobless. I feared that after seeing all of that, he would not be able to photograph me or worse, all of the photos of me would come out distorted because the camera would show the world the "truth" about me. Or perhaps every photo would show the word "FAILURE" stamped across my forehead. Any way this played out in my head, it ended badly. (Note to self: instead of running unlikely scenarios in my head, let's just experience life's scenarios as they happen.)

Geoffrey dropped me off for the photo shoot at the studio that also doubled as the photographer's living quarters at the time. I was so nervous. *This guy is going to be able to see right through me. He is going to know that I am faking my smiles, that I am a failure. Be strong, Mary. These are just pictures. Just be yourself. The worst-case scenario is that you have to retake the photographs.*

A smiling man in his mid-fifties greeted me at the door. He had wispy white hair that was tied back into a ponytail like a more refined hairstyle for Doc Brown in *Back to the Future.* When he introduced himself as Stephen, I couldn't help but notice his thick Boston accent. He was dressed all in black.

Everything was perfect about him: the hair, the black beret, the black clothing, and the accent. He looked every part of a beatnik, but with greater authenticity and warmth. There was absolutely nothing pretentious about him. He wore who he was on his sleeve for the entire world to see, and he did it with such panache and confidence, like it was no big deal. He was so comfortable in his own skin. This was the first time I experienced someone actually living and working in authenticity. Stephen inspired me to want to live in the same real way. I couldn't help but trust him immediately and completely. I heaved a sigh of relief and felt at ease.

As he began the shoot, he commented on how relaxed and comfortable I was in front of the camera. I smiled inside. I was proud of myself and during that time, I forgot about the failure and shame. Stephen helped melt that away, so I was free during that hour to *just be me*. It was so liberating. It was as if this stranger *got* me, as if he could see my true self; there was no judgment rendered, seeing was enough. In those moments, I got to taste my own authenticity; I got to glimpse into the future and see what I could become if I started to live differently.

Stephen and I became friends and helped teach me through his example, patience, and humor how to bring my authenticity to the surface. He lives with near monk-like minimalism by completely intentional choice. With every action he seems to tease and poke fun at the traditional "American Dream," but it is without jeering malice; it is just an unintentional by-product of who he is. He is the most self-less and committed person that I know. When Stephen does something, it is with full effort and energy. I don't think half-assing it is in his genetic makeup. He would instantly give you every last dime and every last possession he had if he believed you would prosper or benefit from its use more than he would.

Stephen seems to have been born with the world's wisdom. He firmly and unapologetically believes that life is too short, so why spend any of it doing something that doesn't make you happy. He can't seem to wrap his head around the fact that most of society is willing to do things that don't make them happy or sacrifice so much precious time in life in the hopes of experiencing a sliver of freedom. This seems absolutely blasphemous and unconventional to him.

I had spent pretty much my entire adult life wasting my time on things that don't make me happy or finding "fixes" that will make my life better "someday." I had seemingly endless justifications for self-inflicted unhappiness and sacrifice. Stephen, on the other hand, didn't see me this way when we first met. He seems to think that I am beautiful inside and am just as genuine and selfless as he is . . . and he is right. It's curious how things seem so obvious to others, yet we struggle sometimes just to see.

Photos plus an amazing friend to show me that it is not only possible, but better to live authentically: priceless and yet, somehow, it only cost me $49.

XIX

HELLO, EMOLECULE

"If you're walking down the right path and you're willing to keep walking, eventually you'll make progress."

BARAK OBAMA

Obviously, we needed money still. This seemed to be the story of our lives. I was a newly licensed attorney but still afraid to fully harness my eMolecule purely based on our dire financial needs. Once we had money, I kept telling myself, I would be able to start a business.

I still believed that getting a job was the answer. I reached out to every law firm in our area. I went to as many free networking events as I could. I applied to at least 250 jobs within a 100-mile radius from where we lived. I shared (some of) my story. I received lots of pity, but pity doesn't pay the bills in case you were wondering. I got a lot of "Oh, well, you seem like a great candidate, but you are very overqualified for this position" or "You have a very impressive resume and would certainly make a great asset to any company. I am sure you will get snapped up by someone soon."

My favorite piece of "career" advice came from a prominent attorney in town. He advised, "You are young. You have your whole life ahead of you. Don't be an attorney. Go find some-thing that will make you happy." Why is this my favorite? Be-cause he was being honest. He saw through my lines of bullshit. He could tell that practicing law was not my true passion. I did not heed his advice because I could only think about one thing: money.

Then, I had my "big break". I had several meetings at a firm near our house. The managing partner and I got along. We worked out a nontraditional arrangement, but at least I would get to use my hard-earned degree. He advised me to come in to the office two weeks later on a Monday morning to solidify the details and I could start working. I was stoked. Things were going to turn around for us. The Friday before I was supposed to start, I called the firm and spoke with the managing partner. "Oh, hi, Mary. I've been wanting to get in contact with you re-garding our arrangement. I've thought about it some more, and we have plenty of work that you could do, but I just don't think I can pay you. Gosh, I'm really sorry." Yep. Sure. Fine. Whatever. Chalk it up to another learning experience.

I learned that if you want to have any say in your future, you don't depend on other people. Job security doesn't exist. I kept getting burned every time I relied on other people to help me start my career. Enough is enough!

I can only take so much rejection. Remember, I am a human. I have feel-ings. I matter, too. Don't you see how hard I have worked just to stay alive, let alone to be where I am today?

I did get a job though. My very first job after becoming a licensed attorney was at Trader Joe's, a grocery store, for $10 an hour. My co-workers were great, but I worked at a grocery store. Swallow that ego. Shed that pride. *Remind me again, Mary, why did you go to law school anyway?* The American Bar Association was right. I was lost. I had strayed from my intended path. I got distracted. I forgot where I was headed.

"I went to law school so I could start my own business and not have to pay an attorney." I responded to myself.

"So why are you working at a grocery store?"
"I don't know. We need money."
"Why haven't you started a business?"
"I don't know what to start."
"Aren't you an attorney?"
"Yes, but I don't want to practice law."
"Maybe you just need to start somewhere. I bet you'd make more than ten dollars an hour."

It was settled then. I was going to start my own law firm. If other people didn't have opportunities for me, I would create them. I'd done it before, so this wasn't anything different. I told my husband. Geoffrey was thrilled. He stood behind me one hundred percent. Wow! He is amazing. I don't know how he puts up with me. I can hardly deal with me and he does it with such patience and grace.

I shared the exciting news with my co-workers at Trader Joe's. They were thrilled too. I don't give them enough credit, but each and every one of them saw something in me that I failed to see: *potential.* My co-workers could not understand why they worked side-by-side with a licensed attorney at a grocery store. Why I didn't move on to something bigger and better. Well, it's because I was lost and I needed them to remind me of that, too. This is truly when I began to realize that I had a gift and in order to give that gift the proper respect it deserved, to nurture it and let it grow into something beautiful, I needed to grab my eMolecule by the proverbial horns!

I can't tell you exactly how long it has been since I worked at Trader Joe's, but it's been awhile. Even to this day, when I go there, I have something akin to celebrity status. The bells at the register start ringing. There are shout-outs: "Mary Todd's in the House!" Hugs come from all directions. Everyone wants an update on the latest chapter of my journey through life.

Why is this? Why did I have such a profound impact on these people? Why do they care about me?

I can't answer those questions because I don't know. That

is my gift I suppose. I am honest and thoughtful. I listened to their problems in the break room. I rendered advice if I could. I gave hugs or empathy if it was needed. I genuinely cared for each and every one of those individuals and something crazy happened: they cared about me in return. I was just being me in all my glory and all my tangled self and they accepted and loved me exactly the way I was. I have tears of gratitude in my eyes right now as I think about all of those faces in their wacky colored tee shirts cheering me on. Sad to see me go, but so happy to see me finally taking flight.

And so my law firm was born. I knew that I was not keen on litigation, so I positioned my firm as peaceful and socially responsible to deter litigious clients. But beyond that initial differentiation, I broke all of the cardinal rules of Successful Business 101. I had no target market, no clearly defined practice areas. I just wanted to help people.

I knew better. I had advised my corporate consulting clients back in the day of these simple, yet egregious errors and yet I committed them myself when the time came to put my knowledge to the test. Despite this rookie mistake, I still got client inquiries. But I had a new problem; the people that needed help couldn't pay for my services. But because I so desperately wanted to help them, I way undervalued my services to make them affordable or I did it for free. Another rookie mistake. But I was helping people, *right?*

Yeah, sort of. But you're not helping yourself either and neither are people lining the streets to help you out. This cannot continue.

The other issue I faced with my firm was that it was structured like a regular, traditional law firm. It resembled nothing like it is today, but rather was an embodiment of everything that I hated about the legal industry. Yes, I had the pretentious professional photo with the pompous and totally boring bio. I used lots of big words to show off my awesomeness. I think the only thing missing was photos of me in front of a lofty looking bookshelf full of matching leather-bound books. It pretty much was completely impersonal and had zero reflection of my beliefs, my values, and me. It wasn't authentic.

I quickly recognized my errors and honed down my practice areas to business law and estate planning, but it was too late to fix all of the problems. I had already taken on matters that I really shouldn't have taken on because they were so time intensive and were not matters that spoke to my interests. As a result, I found myself spread over so many areas of law, that my practice was disjointed and confusing.

I disliked much of the work I had taken on, lots of family law and complex property issues, but I couldn't say no, which really wasn't helping anyone's situation. I didn't have my heart in the issues, so I wasn't serving those clients as well as someone who did have their heart in the game. But it's okay, because at least I started. For the first time in my life, I was letting my eMolecule guide me instead of trying to force myself onto a path.

In retrospect, whenever I followed my entrepreneurial spirit, my eMolecule, my path was clear and I experienced greater satisfaction and fulfillment in whatever I was doing. It's when I gave into distraction, temptation, or forced my head to separate from my heart that I found myself in places of darkness and unhappiness.

Following your eMolecule takes commitment, strong courage of conviction and passion. It isn't easy. You have to admit things to yourself and you have to sacrifice things. You have to remain true to yourself. You will face temptation, but hold steadfast. This is one of those "Do as I say, not as I do" moments. I faced temptation and I fell prey to its seduction.

XX

TRICKED INTO BITING THE POISON APPLE

"The biggest human temptation is to settle for too little."

THOMAS MERTON

Be careful what you wish for. I wanted desperately to feel like I wasn't missing out on a part of the world: namely the part of the world that had a job. Although I had started a law firm, we had no money to put toward marketing and those first clients that did come in were not in the best position to pay. We needed money so desperately; we were willing to do almost anything. I, again, was willing to sacrifice my eMolecule, what I knew was my path and true destiny, for what seemed like the greater good of both of us, for money. I was going to solve our money issues forever and a job was going to be the answer!

I succumbed to the temptation of money and got a coveted job interview. I remember the interview like it was yesterday. I was nervous and excited because I knew the future of our bank account depended on it. I was nervous because I knew I really didn't want to be there, but I tried to ignore that pesky little feeling inside. I walked into a lofty looking office building and headed up to the sixth floor. The hallways were dimly lit with high efficiency florescent lighting. Mass-produced art masquerading as original handmade canvases hung on the walls lining the corridor. I felt flooded with light as the door opened and I was greeted with natural light pouring in from the windows lining the back office wall. I was shown into the general counsel's office.

General Counsel was a tall slender man. He wore a faux Burberry dress shirt with French cuffs tucked into a pair of jeans for the interview (versus my very smart navy gabardine suit with silk ruffled blouse. That dissention would set the tone for our entire professional relationship). Everything about him seemed awkward; the way he clumsily shuffled his feet to close the door behind me, how he failed to make eye contact with me during the interview, oh, and the excruciatingly long silences where it was unclear whether he was reading an email, forgot my presence, or was trying to think of what to say next. My interview began with me initiating the conversation. I sat there quietly across from him at his desk while I experienced my first of many of these long pauses. When I had had enough, I started to speak.

"So, I see you are from New York. How long have you been in Florida?"

"About two years."

"Great! Me too. I love it down here. The weather is amazing, and oh! that sand at the beaches."

"Yeah, I guess so . . ." he trailed off, leading into more awkward silence.

The interview progressed at about that same slow pace for the greater part of an hour. I believe he was reading the interview questions right from his computer screen. It was one of the least interesting and most impersonal experiences I have ever really experienced.

My father-in-law was in town visiting us. When I returned home, he asked, "So, how was it?"

"It was one of the most boring hours of my life. I would rather eat glass than have to sit through another hour with that guy. There is absolutely no way I can take that job if they offer it to me."

Ah, how time makes the heart forgetful! A week later, I took the job despite all of the alarm bells and warning whistles going off in my head and despite my statement to the contrary.

In my adult life, there are two things that I have come to despise: complacency and inefficiency. Complacency and inefficiency are best friends, wherever you find one, you will find the other. Together they breed low morale, wasted resources, and can rot an organization (or home) from the inside out, just like rust slowly feeding off of and eventually taking over metal.

On my first day at the office, I walked right into the face of chaos, at least by my standards. The entire environment, despite assurances from the CEO promising that the corporate culture was one that supported innovation, was a full on, festering breeding ground for inefficiency and complacency, as well as a few of their other friends: poor leadership, lack of accountability, zero cross-training, and little to no documented processes or guidelines.

It was a virtual free-for-all in the department that I would head. I was put in charge of running a legal department staffed with people that had virtually no legal experience, but it wasn't their fault. They had been thrown to the wolves and were merely fending for themselves. I felt bad for these individuals, who worked with such forlorn faces, they carried so much stress it was palpable, hanging like a thick, sticky cloud over their desks.

No, this is not fair. We need tools, processes, and resources. This isn't a team. We must come together as a team and I can lead them. I have to lead them. I will lead them.

My first order of business was to interview each person on my new team to find out what processes each had created to complete the same tasks. Together, we created a uniform set of standards and processes to reduce redundancy and error rates. We completely overhauled the system: changing how tasks were delegated, creating a system for accountability, and cross training to increase workload flexibility. So in reality, it wasn't quite that easy because I had to fight tooth and nail for resources for my people over *everything*.

One of the first things I asked for from General Counsel was a dry erase board and easel to put in the department for tracking task completion, providing updates, posting reminders, and creating inspiration. He one hundred percent disagreed with me, stating that to post that type of information would only create dissent amongst the team, breed discontentment by creating a competitive "sales-y" environment, and basically do the exact opposite of each of my goals. I ordered the dry erase board anyway.

I should interject here that lawyers make notoriously bad managers and business people. Why? Because they have been trained to be lawyers, not managers and most know nothing about running a business despite the fact that many lawyers set out their own shingle, starting up their own law practice. (hmmmm . . . perhaps there is a correlation between the number of small practices that fail and little to no business training . . . serious shortcomings of the traditional law school model, that is a soapbox for another day my friends.) Suffice it to say, General Counsel epitomized a stereotypical attorney attempting to manage.

It was clear from that very first meeting regarding the dry erase board how my superior perceived me. I would never get the respect that I deserved or expected from a fellow member of the Bar. He was not a team player and not a good leader. He was the worst kind of leader actually; the kind that wants to be in charge and maintain power, but do the least amount of work possible. Leadership is work.

Communication with General Counsel was tenuous, if not impossible. I would raise a personnel issue or seek his feedback or advice on a matter, and if I got a response at all, it typically came in the form of "I started to read your email, but then deleted it. I assumed you were just having a moment of weakness . . ." Needless to say, most of the meetings between us were

wrought with tension. They were either full of disrespectful berating toward any ideas or proposals for change that I concocted
or a barrage of pointed questions over some incident that, by
the time General Counsel stepped out of his ivory tower and
caught wind of it, was already diffused or resolved and neatly
wrapped up. His chauvinism rendered me speechless on many
occasions.

I thought this organization was supposed to support and reward innovation? The CEO professed his extreme distaste for
complacency. I was hired to create change and promised that I
would not rest on my laurels, but soon realized that this would
be a solo crusade. Less than one month into my new role, I went
rogue. It was my personal crusade, despite any consequences
that I suffered, to provide my team with the tools they needed
for success. I would lead them and support them regardless of
the lack of support I received from General Counsel.

I instituted Mary's School of Law, an eight-week educational
program about the litigation process, so everyone had the same
understanding of legal process and procedure. At the end, there
was a bar exam. We played silly legal vocabulary games. I was
candid and transparent in my policies. Every Monday morning
we would meet around the dry erase board and discuss issues
and events from the previous week and get ready to tackle new
ones. I would call mysterious meetings in the conference room
with silly meeting titles, like "Breakfast for dinner? No, I'll take
dessert for breakfast" to pique interest and intrigue. Sometimes
the meetings were very serious, regarding compliance breach-
es and other times it was simply a ten-minute break to relax,
take a breather, and reconnect over popsicles during a stressful
week. We had fun, but not at the expense of our performance.
We were a team where everyone was equal. If someone made
a mistake, we all stood behind that mistake and learned from it,
instead of pointing fingers and dodging blame.

My team was amazing. They loved me, and the feeling was
mutual. Yes, we had our rough patches and obstacles, but for the

most part, we were a cohesive bunch. For some, I became more than a manager. I became a mentor and for me that hit a sweet spot. I realized that I inspired these individuals to work harder, yes, but I inspired them to reach for new dreams that they hadn't thought possible for themselves before. I realized I could change lives. This is what made me show up every day. Believing in these individuals and nurturing them so they could grow gave me such fulfillment. I was starting to truly step into my strength and own my path. However, it was evident that the equilibrium was off, the environment was all wrong for me to grow, and I was going to be paying the price.

PART THREE

XXI

YOGA

"A soul mate is the one person whose love is powerful enough to motivate you to meet your soul, to do the emotional work of self-discovery, of awakening."

KENNY LOGGINS

I hated everything. I hated my job. I hated my life. I was so full of negativity, it began to weigh heavily on my marriage. Have you heard the saying that after a rough day at the office, you "go home and kick the dog?" It basically means that you come home frustrated and angry and beat your dog to blow off steam and release tension. Yeah, pretty nasty stuff, and I was doing it, except we don't have a dog. In my case, I would come home and kick my husband. And It. Was. Ugly.

Why would you take out so much anger and negativity on the one person that you never want to hurt, Mary? He doesn't deserve this. He is so loving and supportive. He is amazing, in fact. You're just driving him away. You're going to mess this up and you won't get a second chance . . .

And then the rant would begin. Profanity, berating, accusations, and assumptions, all of it came darting out of my mouth with such accuracy and precision to target my sweet, sweet husband with maximum damage.

One day, he'd had enough. He had politely advised me on several occasions of his disdain for my post-work belittling sessions, but that clearly hadn't worked. I walked in the door, dropped my bag next to the sofa and slipped out of my heels. I was about to begin, but he stopped me short. In fact, my mouth was open, jaw dropped and poised to spit poisonous darts and retort at my first chance.

"STOP! Before you say anything, just stop. I need you to listen to me and not interrupt me. I know that's hard for you, but I need this. I can't—I can NOT see you when you come home from work. You need to go somewhere else first. Maybe you should get a hobby or something, but you need to do something in between work and home. I am not your punching bag. I will listen when you need me to listen, but you're mean. You're spiteful and angry. You hurt me every day."

My jaw was permanently dropped open, but I was no longer poised to retaliate; I was speechless.

He continued, "I love you and I will always love you, but you make it so difficult sometimes to allow me to love you. I need you to respect that. I know you love me too, but you're not showing it very well. Please go get a hobby. Do something so *this* doesn't happen." He waved his hands around in an erratic manner simulating my complete, crazy person tirade.

I know this doesn't seem like a black Pontiac moment, but it was, and in the worst kind of way because this time, I truly stood to lose everything. All of the other moments in my life, I knew I would be hurting people close to me and I would be hurting myself, but the decisions I made were to keep me protected from more harm but still leave me with a tiny little leg to stand on. If I lost Geoffrey, I would lose all of my love and our dreams, which entailed living life together. With no Geoffrey, living life would mean living solo, and that for me would be a deal breaker. We are integral to each other's existence, so if I lost him I would have nothing left to live for. *Nothing.* The slightest hint of the possibility of losing my soul mate is just too much to bear.

I swallowed hard and choked down my tears, but it all came out, messy, snotty soul-shuddering sobs of grief, loss, and guilt. And, yeah, all of this emotion came up just from the mere hint of a slight possibility of driving away the most important person in my life. No, losing Geoffrey was not an option if I wanted to keep my sanity and my life.

That night I couldn't sleep. Those nasty voices in my head came back. They were swirling around and screaming too much for me to actually hear any one particular voice. I felt like I was losing control again. I wept silently while looking over at my sleeping husband. I had flashbacks to a time when he didn't occupy that side of the bed.

It made me chuckle as I recalled the small war that waged every evening when he first started to claim that side of the bed. You see, Chester used to sleep on what is now Geoffrey's pillow and our other cat, Elliott, would sleep under the blankets cuddled into my abdomen. When Geoffrey arrived, there was a pretty serious turf war with Chester. Chester was afraid for me. He protected me as best a cat could. He knew I needed him. I needed him to wrap his paws around my hand or cuddle his face into them while we slept, so I wouldn't feel alone. He wasn't ready to trust Geoffrey with his delicate momma, so he resisted Geoffrey until he felt I was safe. Chester would plop down on Geoffrey's face in the middle of the night or paw aggressively at his neck to keep him awake warning him that he was not welcome to get too comfortable next to me. Sometimes Chester would position himself on the pillows between the two of us, like a chaperone at a junior high dance making sure we wouldn't get too close. Finally, Chester surrendered. I guess he could sense that Geoffrey would do anything to protect me and keep me safe, and probably do a better job than a cat. Chester sensed that I felt safe, so he could rest easy.

No, going back to an empty bed was not an option. Chester wouldn't be able to protect me again. We had all grown too accustomed to Geoffrey's warmth and presence, his snoring in the night and his flatulence in the morning or pressing my face into his chest if my thoughts kept me awake at night. I shuddered at the thought of not having him next to me. I needed a hobby, and fast.

About a year prior, a close friend had given me a free pass to a local yoga studio, probably when I needed it most, but I was too chicken to walk in the door and give it a try. Now, it was like my golden ticket outta cloudy Crazy Town. I had tried yoga at home a few times, but it would be a gross understatement to even call me a novice.

I mustered up the courage to walk in the doors to the studio and immediately I felt safe. The way the studio smelled, the lighting, the warmth, and the sincerity of the people working there. Remember that laboratory that I would retreat to when I was a janitor? I had that same sense of safety, but here, people, a community, surrounded me instead of just reduced-particle air and machinery. I fumbled my way around on my yoga mat for several classes, sticking to the back corner of the room pretending that no one could see me. The truth was people could see me, but they weren't looking at me. They didn't care. They were too involved in their own yoga practice and working through their own issues on their mat to even give me an ounce of attention or care if I couldn't do a pose.

Day after day and week after week, I showed up on my mat with all of my baggage after work, but before I went home to see my Geoffrey. There were some days on my mat where I had such poignant moments it would bring me to tears in the middle of class and all I could do was lay on the floor in child's pose and sob. Other days, I came with anger and frustration and I would move through my practice stomping and kicking my mat. Two things started happening: first, I had the honest realization that the only person judging me at the yoga studio was myself. I started to become self-aware in a more responsible way. Second, when I would come home from the studio, Geoffrey would ask me how my day was. "I don't remember how work went, but I know I love you," I would respond, beaming with love and admiration for my husband.

In the style of yoga that I practice, Baptiste Power Vinyasa, we are asked really only to do three things: (1) show up and be present to ourselves and our practice, (2) breathe, and (3) set an intention of possibility for our practice. Starting out, showing up and being present was a challenge. I wasn't used to actually being in the moment. In fact, most of my life was spent trying to outrun the past while planning or worrying about the future. Just existing and being in the moment was not a part of my life. With practice, patience, and discipline, I began to learn how to just exist wherever it was that I stood. I wasn't allowed to judge me in that place because standing in that exact spot is exactly where I needed to be in that very moment. If it's beautiful, then revel in it and savor it. If it's ugly, then be aware of its ugliness and messiness. You need to have both in order to achieve balance, both mentally and physically. Sometimes, presence is the best I can do on and off my mat and I still struggle with staying present, but it's a practice after all.

Turns out that breathing is the most important physiological act our amazing bodies perform. Our breath sucks in the world outside. We need the outside world to sustain our physical presence. Without it, we would suffocate, no matter how polluted, chaotic or scary it seems. Our breath is a simple act that usually takes place unconsciously, under our radar.

Try becoming conscious of your breath; close your eyes and focus on your breath: *feel it*. When I close my eyes and feel my breath, an amazing thing happens. My breath deepens; I start to feel the gentle rise and fall of my chest and belly like the ebb and flow of gentle waves lapping on a beach. I feel my body, what it feels like to be inside of me. Inside of me seems like a complicated, messy place with lots of dark corners, but when I breathe, all of the corners become filled with light and my mind quiets itself. Things aren't as complicated anymore. Things aren't ugly and chaotic; they are beautiful. A transformation takes place when you become aware of your breath. You become aware of your existence and your proximity to life around you. The simple act of conscious breathing brings into focus all of the simple pleasures and simple beauty that surrounds us each and every day. It is my "stop and smell the roses" time when I remind myself to slow down and savor the moments. It gives me permission to stop and watch a lizard scurry across the sidewalk in front of my toes or soak up the verdant velvety leaves of a plant I haven't seen before. Breathing gives me permission to exist.

When I first began my yoga practice, each time I practiced I dedicated my practice to my husband. It was my intention to shine all of my love and gratitude toward him as a "Thank You" for being so patient and so supportive. Doing so expanded my heart more and more and I tapped into greater adoration and a level of love for him that is so deep, it is indescribable. It is what I imagine a parent must feel when a child is born. A type of love that is honestly unconditional and wholly irrevocable, probably irrational, too. I didn't know this type of love existed and I certainly never thought it was something I was capable of. This is a beautiful thing, but I was shining out for someone else. I still needed to learn how to shine for myself, to love myself in the same deep way that I discovered I love Geoffrey.

I started to dedicate my practice to myself. It was hard. I realized how much easier it seems to be to do the work for someone else, to turn the focus and attention away from myself. Showing up on my mat was a sign of selfish gratitude, an act that was me showing respect and thanks for *myself.* Loving yourself with the same deep love that you share with your spouse or children is difficult. It is laden with guilt and self-loathing. It is selfish and that word has a bad rap.

Why is it that when we are being selfish it makes us feel badly? Why don't we grant ourselves the same permission to love ourselves and devote time to growing that love?

Because we are taught not to give ourselves that permission. We are taught about service and about being selfless. These are good values, we should always be willing to reach out and help those in need, but when are we allowed to reach in and help ourselves, too? They don't talk about that in school. That is selfish, which is erroneously synonymized with self-serving, and we are told this is bad so we begin to feel guilty when we do things purely for ourselves.

Over time, we learn to avoid the guilt because nobody likes feeling guilty by avoiding doing things that serve only us. This is all fine and dandy, except that we as individuals, too, are important and just as we may be willing and ready to reach out to someone else in need, that feeling may not be reciprocated when we need it the most. Or worse, we are afraid to ask for help because that seems selfish, so no one reaches out to help us when we need it because no one knows we need help! Phew! That's deep.

When we begin to be honest with ourselves, we are honest with others. We are surrounded by people who love us and who are willing to support us, but we need to give ourselves permission to not feel guilty when we need something. It isn't self-serving. It isn't a sign of weakness. It isn't being selfish (in a bad way). It is a sign of being human. You are showing others that you love yourself. Swallow. Breathe. I told you this was hard.

I want to remind you that this is an ongoing practice. I didn't just magically start loving myself. I still don't magically love myself, but I practice; I try.

One of the things that I love about my yoga practice is the physical manifestation of progress. When you begin a mental exercise, like trying to learn to love yourself, it is hard to quantify what the initial state is or track the progress along the way. However, when dealing with the physical, it is easier to know what point A looks like versus the current location. For example, when I began my practice, I wasn't physically strong enough to do a pose called chaturanga dandasana. It is a transitional pose integral to the practice of yoga where you essentially hover your body in a plank position inches off the floor like the bottom portion of a push up, with your elbows tucked in closely to your body at a ninety-degree angle. It is hard. It takes patience, practice, and strength. Mine were not pretty. I collapsed and flopped all over the floor, bracing myself with my knees or my abdomen as my strength was building. Then, it happened. I did it. I became strong enough to do a chaturanga dandasana without training wheels! I was months into my practice before I had this revelatory manifestation of physical success. My persistence and practice built strength.

Two things happened after this achievement. First, I realized that this physical manifestation of success was tracking along with the mental progress I was making. Although it was harder for me to see that progress, I could *feel* the progress being made internally. My external yoga practice reaffirmed and reminded me that I, too, was making progress inside. Second, I was aware that I was the one who made it possible. It was *my* work, *my* strength, *my* patience that compounded on itself to display this physical act of triumph. This rang true with the emotional and spiritual progress that *I did.* No one else could show up on my mat for me and make me stronger. I began to feel self-worth. I began to reevaluate my life and reprioritize my definition of success. I began to realize that the answer to fulfillment and happiness was already inside me. I needed to love, cherish, and honor my eMolecule.

XXII

IF I MUST CHOOSE,
I CHOOSE ME OVER THEE

"Success means having the courage, the determination, and the will to become the person you believe you were meant to be."

GEORGE SHEEAN

I have a confession to make. I'm rich and I'm successful. And I'm not talking about a little bit rich—I am filthy rich. Yes, it's true. Instead of being jealous though, I want you to join me.

It's funny how when we say the word success, the first thought that pops into our heads relates to money. Why is this? I do not necessarily believe that money is the root of all evil, and I also don't believe it defines our success, but I do believe it is easy to forget this. So we focus on the money. After all, it is tangible and no matter how much of it we have (or don't have), it always pretends to whisper to us that if we had just a little bit more, life would be just a little bit easier. We've all heard the saying "Money can't buy you happiness," but yet we continue to put all of our efforts and emphasis on money. Well, what if I told you that I have had lots of money, but the money didn't make me successful. I was not okay. Things on their face may have seemed perfect. Some of my co-workers would comment on my fearlessness or confidence and my perfect marriage. HA! If they only knew how often Geoffrey and I were really hanging onto our sanity sometimes by just a thread or how frequently I battled with myself to calm my fears or force "happiness."

Success doesn't happen to us. Money doesn't make us successful. *We create our own success.* And much like entrepreneurship, you get to choose the definition. How do you want to define yourself? How do you want to define success?

One day, I had a revelation: *I am not two people. There is no such thing as "work Mary" and "any other time Mary." I am just one person.* I kept trying and trying to compartmentalize who I am. I was forcing myself to show up to a job, which I hated, swallow my instincts and squelch my eMolecule all in the name of money. Then, after work I would head to my yoga mat and try to detoxify all of my "work Mary" out of me, so I could be "normal Mary" at home for the rest of the day. This is pretty much the equivalent of putting a Band-Aid on a broken arm. It may only provide a teensy bit of mental relief, but actually does nothing to heal the problem. I should also add that it. is. exhausting.

I sat in my cubicle at the office and looked around. It looked the same way I felt: grey and gloomy. The cubicle was upholstered in grey fabric, the office furniture was grey, the carpeting yet another shade of grey, the walls were painted grey, and, alas, it was cloudy outside. I heaved a heavy sigh and stared at my email inbox, with new emails piling up one on top of the other.

"Ugh. What am I doing here? I can't do this. I thought I could stick with this. It's just a job."

"Yeah, but it's starting to define you. Why are you here? Is this where you always dreamed you would be?"

"No, but we need to have money."

"Are you happy?"

"No."

"So clearly money is not the answer. What about taking the plunge on one of those business ideas you have? I know you sit here daydreaming about them. This isn't feeding your soul. Remember, you are worth more than this.

Have you learned nothing from yoga?"

"Yeah but it is safe here."

"Is it? Think about what you're willing to lose, what you are willing to risk losing. Money is coming to you at the cost of your husband, your happiness, and the dream that you two share. None of these have anything to do with money. Are you willing to lose any one of those things"

"No."

"If you lose one of these things, what will happen?"

"I will have regrets."

"What is your favorite mantra"

"To live with no regrets."

"Then what are you doing here?"

"I . . . I . . . I don't know. I can't be here anymore. I will miss my team. I love to lead and inspire them."

Instead of responding to the mounting emails in my inbox, I promptly drafted my letter of resignation. I marched into General Counsel's office with such resolve, he had no choice but to give me his attention. My heart was beating faster than a snare drum and my eMolecule was on fire. Energy and excitement coursed through my veins. I could hardly sit still in the seat across from his desk.

"General Counsel," I began, "Thank you for this opportunity. I have learned so much about myself here: who I am and who I want to be. From that self-inquiry, I recognize that this is not the right environment for me to grow and be nurtured. I will truly miss leading my team, but it is in my best interest to leave. "

He sat frozen, staring at me blankly like a deer stunned by a set of headlights before his thoughts could catch up with his words. "Wow! This is really unexpected. Are you not happy here? Is there some sort of problem? What are you going to do?"

"Yes, I am unhappy here. I have expressed that to you before, but this is different. I can't really explain it. I know I just have to leave. I don't think you would understand if I tried to explain it to you."

"Umm . . . okay . . . well, what are you going to do? Do you have another job offer?"

"No. I don't really know what I am going to do. I just have to follow my heart and trust it to lead me. Again, thank you for this opportunity."

I rose from the chair and glided out of his office. I felt so tall, almost invincible. I wanted to yell out to the world about my triumph! *I did it!!!* This was it. This is what I had always wanted to do and I was *finally* strong enough to trust myself and just do it. I was going to start my own business. I finally embraced my eMolecule (ten years after discovering it, but, eh, who's counting anyway?).

Embracing your eMolecule means you must redefine success. It's not about money. It's about the richness of the life you live as defined by your relationships and listening to your heart. Your heart will tell you where your passions truly lie and your eMolecule will help give you the courage to enterprise your passion into something beautiful and unique, BUT you must bring your entire self and be willing to give your entire self. Nothing less, but nothing more.

We all have a story because we all have experienced life in some way, shape, or form. Our lives are a product of our choices. We choose to be where we are every moment of the day. Sometimes we put ourselves in lousy places, but other times, breathtaking places. But all moments begin with a choice. Choosing is the first step to becoming successful.

If you are sitting somewhere right now that you hate, choose to not be there. As you look at your life, look at the things that are actually serving you versus the things that you think are serving you. If you are doing things that don't serve you, then choose to stop doing those things. Be selfish and choose yourself. It shouldn't be a hard choice, but choosing ourselves is so difficult for some reason. Maybe we think we don't deserve it. Or maybe we don't choose ourselves because we think we are supposed to act in a certain way or be doing certain things. Well, if you choose to stay in that place, then you will not be successful.

I hate to spoil it, but it's true.

Success for me is having the ability to slow down, to ride my bike to the beach or to the grocery store or to stop and smell a beautiful flower (as cliché as that is). Being able to slow down has strengthened my relationships too, and those have made me rich. I am rich because I love and I am loved in return. I am loved just the way I am . . . cowering in a corner in my bathroom or on stage before an audience of several hundred. In both moments, I am beautiful and genuine. I am authentic. (And if you're taking notes, authenticity is another one of those secret ingredients).

A crazy thing happened when I started to choose me and only do things that served me. Well, actually a few crazy things happened. One, stress vanished. I now joke with people when they talk about stress and quip, "Yeah, stress. I gave that up for Lent a few years ago." Two, I was able to experience love differently, more fully. Three, I became waaaaaaaay happier. I cannot overstate the increased level of happiness. And finally, I started to become fulfilled. For me, no amount of money or tangible riches could ever lure me away from these feelings. Once you harness your eMolecule and you are able to taste this freedom of success, you will understand too.

My mother once wrote to me in a letter: "The key to success is recognizing your own potential and creating life's opportunities . . . Embrace your dream!" This, my friends, is what success is about. Giving yourself permission to go out there and live your dream to be anything you want to be. *Being okay with you where you are, who you are, and recognizing that if you want to create change in your life, it begins with you: loving yourself and telling yourself that you are amazing—and believing it.*

XXIII

THE CATHYS

"There are only two mistakes one can make along the road to truth. Not going all the way, and not starting."

BUDDHA

There will always be people in your life that envy you. Not in a hateful or spiteful way, but people who wish they were more like you because they believe that they will never, ever be able to be like you. It is just simply unattainable for them. I call these people, the Cathys.

I have a very good friend whose name is Cathy. Cathy and I used to be work colleagues; now we are close friends. Cathy is beautiful, bright, and intelligent, but she sees herself as frumpy, stupid, and uninspired. She is a doubter in every sense of the word, paralyzed by risk and fear to take a step in even the slightest direction to the left or the right. In fact, most of the time she is just standing still and screaming inside at herself for not being good enough and at the world for being such a seemingly tough place for her to exist.

When we worked together, and even now, she responds to my stories of trial, tribulation, and triumph with a heavy heave and a "Yeah, but you're so smart/confident/fearless/[insert any adjective that describes a positive attribute here]. I could never do that. I'm not [insert whatever adjective was just used here] enough." You see, the Cathys (and maybe you are one) have such little confidence in themselves that they are hopelessly ignorant to the fact that confidence is learned. It comes from lots and lots of practice.

I write this not because I am judging Cathy or her choices, but because she inspires me to work harder and, for that, my heart goes out to her. I want to gather up all of the Cathys, shake them by their shoulders and yell, "Wake UP! Wa-a-a-ake U-P! Today is the day that you are going to begin feeling. Waking up is the hardest part. Today the work begins, but don't be afraid. Don't you see, we are just the same, you and me? I have stood in your shoes. I have been afraid to even put my shoes on let alone take a step in any direction. You put your shoes on every day! Don't you see what an accomplishment that is? Don't you see how much further along it puts your start from mine? When you wake up and put on your shoes, recognize it. Acknowledge yourself for it. It is brave. It means you are not giving up, not today. Today I put my shoes on! Today I am ready to open my eyes! Today I will let myself experience emotion. Today I will feel life! And Cathy, I still get afraid every day, but I have learned to overcome it. I am not whatever you have conjured me up as in your mind. I know what those first steps feel like, but I can't take them for you. This is your journey on your path. You will have to do the work for yourself, but I am here."

Oh God, here we go-o-o-o-o . . . my heart flutters and jumps out of my chest. I close my eyes because for some reason, it is just better to try and not see what you are about to face, even if it is beautiful. My throat becomes dry and it is next to impossible to swallow. My stomach summersaults inside and I immediately regret that I ate anything for breakfast.

"Here, grab my hand, Cathy." *I am so scared, Cathy, and I know you are, too.* "Let's hold hands and take this first step together. This is the worst part: that first step." *Trust me. I know.* "Today, you take your first step. Don't worry about or think about tomorrow. It is still today. Revel in it. Be in it. We will worry about tomorrow when it comes, but not right now. Stay brave today. One day at a time."

By the way, that's all anyone asks of you and it's all you should ask from yourself. Remember Alice and the White Rabbit in Wonderland? Remember what the White Rabbit said to Alice? "Sometimes forever lasts just a second." A second isn't scary. It isn't even a blip on the radar. Just remember that as you take first steps every day. Each time you take these first steps, they get easier and easier each time as you move further away from the starting line.

And always know that you will never be alone on your journey. I am here. We are here. We will support you. We will catch you if you trip. We will spin you around if you start heading in the wrong direction. Just please take my hand. Just take your first step. It doesn't have to be big. You just have to take it.

"Cathy, don't you see how far you have come since our first encounter? Remember when you were afraid to make a ripple in the water? Now you make waves! You make choices! You lead people and they follow! I know as I say this to you, you are shaking your head as if I lie to you. You sit in disagreement about how amazing you are. You must discover this on your own. To this I tell you the following: When you are feeling lonely, go find someone that is in need of love. Share your love with them and neither of you will be lonely. When you feel helpless, go find someone who needs help. Help them. When you feel like crying, cry. Then get up, put your shoes on, go outside and smile at a stranger. Say 'Hello' if you can muster the courage to speak. Then, you will begin to see that you are enough. You will see what I see. You will see the real you. You will see that your real you is stunning and powerful. Do this and you will discover this for yourself."

When I met Cathy, my first impression was that she is incredibly pensive and guarded. She avoided confrontation and would seem to back down at the first sign of tension. She was afraid to speak her mind or share her ideas. She consistently put the needs and wants of others above her own. She was exhausted. I could see so much potential in her, but no one had given her a place to grow and thrive. Maybe I saw myself when I looked at her. Maybe I had flashbacks and saw a lost girl sitting in a college classroom fumbling around for her future before an angel Professor would provide her with perfect growing conditions. I wanted to be her professor. I wanted to help her blossom.

Now Cathy is a bud, slowly getting bigger and opening up to the possibility of her potential. She will bloom someday when she realizes that she has always been ready. Perhaps I will be able to help her see this or she will be strong enough to do it on her own. Now, this brings us to the problem with the Cathys. They always seem to have excuses that usually involve money or timing or cowardice. It doesn't really matter; it's all just fear and self-doubt rearing its ugly little head. Most of the justifications are surrounding a false sense of security anyway.

Why do you keep going to that job you hate? Because you need the money? What you're really saying is that you think money is more important than your current happiness. Well, when that someday happens and you have all the money you wanted to stash away and hoard, please call me and let me know if you are finally happy. I'm going to go out on a limb and say "no." Because by the time that day comes (and it will never come), you will have sacrificed everything else in your life that is important to you: your family, your health, and your relationships. So ask yourself if money is really what's holding you back.

The other thing about "jobs" is that they entail working for someone else. The Cathys hate bosses, but yet seem to think that they lack the ability to be their own boss due to low self-esteem and because starting their own venture is "too risky." This makes no sense to me because if money is, in fact, the all important thing that the Cathys need in order to survive, then why would you trust someone else to provide it for you? If you're on the job and something needs to be completed ASAP and be 100% perfect, who do you trust? The answer: no one but yourself. You do the task yourself because that is the only way you will know, with actual certainty that the job got done the right way. Am I right? Yeah. You're welcome. Stop beating around the bush and go pick up your eMolecule, dust it off, give it a big hug and kiss, and use it.

Cathys also render big judgments on others and on themselves. I am anti-judgment (on a perfect day, which also never happens), but honestly we all judge. It's part of our human makeup. In pure biological terms, it is how we decide whom to associate with or mate with. All animals judge. They judge for survival. We judge for survival and to make us feel better about the choices we've made. Judgment allows us to discern one human from another or from a different mammal species altogether. It is our best friend and our worst enemy on a bad hair day. We can feel lofty and laugh at other people who are having a worse hair day than us and be angry with those experiencing a better hair day. Judgment can also foster camaraderie. All of us bad-hair-day-ers can band together and hate on the good-hair-day-ers. But really? Does this really make anyone feel better? No. It's more of that superficial impulse-purchase-happiness that is fleeting and then leaves us feeling even worse.

Then there is the worst kind of judgment, when you judge yourself. Why is this the worst kind? Because, believe it or not, the world does not stop and start on my whim or yours, for that matter, and despite what you or I may think, neither of us is the center of the universe, yet most of the judgment we render is on ourselves and no one in the world actually notices your good hair day or bad hair day. And, Gasp! if they do notice, I promise you that the status of your hair will not derail their entire day, only yours. So do yourself a favor and "fuhgettaboutit" because everyone else already has.

I used to think that there were types of people: those with the eMolecule and those without it. That was before I realized everyone has it. Anyone has the ability to harness one's entrepreneurial spirit. All of us have the ability to achieve our dreams and live out our purpose through our passions. There are not two types of people; we are not divided by the haves and have-nots. We are just simply in two different places: the ones that have acknowledged and embraced their eMolecules and the ones that have not yet discovered or choose to ignore their eMolecules. Neither place is the right place or the wrong place. Whatever pack you find yourself in is exactly where you need to be in this moment, but know that moments change. Our needs change. I, myself, have danced back and forth between these two. There is truly only one thing that moves us across from one side to the other: the decision to act.

"So, Cathy, W-A-K-E U-P! Show the world that today is the day. Show us that today you will act. Show yourself. You're not right if you do or wrong if you don't. Remember, these are just moments. They are small; they are fleeting, but the aggregate of what choices you make in these moments move you forward. Yes, if you miss this moment, there will be another one, but if you miss too many moments regret will find you." *Regret. Regret is not your friend. Yes, he can be your teacher, but you can't learn if you don't move.*

"Choose to act. Choose now."

XXIV

EMBRACING THE "E"

"I used to dream about escaping my ordinary life, but my life was never ordinary. I had simply failed to notice how extraordinary it was."

RANSOM RIGGS,
Miss Peregrine's Home for Peculiar Children

One week after choosing me and leaving my job, I had registered a new corporation, signed a lease, and was well on my way to opening a retail sunglass boutique. It was awesome. Business startup is seriously like a drug to me. It gives me such a buzz of energy and makes me high on possibilities. It is the best thrill I have ever gotten, and I know a thing or two about that.

Why sunglasses, you ask? At no point prior to this moment have I expressed any interest in sunglasses to you, and you're saying to yourself, "She said passion was a key factor in a successful enterprise." Yes, yes I did. A sunglass boutique, though not my passion, involves conceptualizing, creating, and developing a business venture, which is right up my alley. I chose sunglasses so I could just dip my toe in to test out the waters. I mean I live on the coast in Southwest Florida. Everybody needs sunglasses every day and there are lots of cash-happy tourists, so it's pretty much a no-brainer. And I did my research; sunglasses have one of the highest retail markups. These factors made me feel confident that I was appropriately mitigating my risk.

I know there are still some doubters out there asking, "Isn't starting up your own business expensive? I'd never have that kind of money to risk." Let me be honest here. I started my business with $5,000 compliments of my VISA credit card. Yup, folks. Good old-fashioned credit card financing. Worst case scenario: I would pay the minimum payments until I'm old and grey and it would end up costing me $17,000 or something like that over the course of my lifetime. However ,the reward, even if the business wasn't profitable, is that I had done it. I tried it. I would never have that *I wish I had . . .* sort of thinking. *No regrets.* That, to me, is priceless.

I was in my element. Designing the layout, hunting for suppliers, developing my marketing mix. If I could start a business every week, I would. I. LOVE. IT. After several weeks of putting it all together and completing my build-out, it was opening day! I was on cloud nine. I absolutely did not care one bit that I had no customers. I was able to be out there, doing my own thing, meeting and talking to new people. It was awesome! But this book isn't about building a successful business; it's about looking into yourself and finding the moxy to embrace your entrepreneurial spirit.

The universe is a funny place. Usually, it makes no sense and it leaves us scratching our heads wondering, "WTF? What just happened?" or "Why is this happening to me?" That being said, the universe always seems to send you a helper just when you need one—just when you are beginning to doubt yourself. Remember, if you trust yourself and the universe, it will provide you everything you need. But man, sometimes keeping the faith is *so* hard.

As shocking as this may sound, I enjoyed selling sunglasses because it gave me an opportunity to meet people, connect with them, and educate them even if the education was as trivial as explaining to them what color lenses are most appropriate for their lifestyle or activities. (It sounds so simple now when I write that down, but it was a long time in the making to boil down the pieces of the retail sunglass business that I *really* liked.)

As fun as it was and as much as I loved the startup process, I felt that I was not serving my greater purpose, so I was still left unfulfilled. My old enemies, fear and self-doubt, crept in and I began to doubt the choices I'd made regarding opening my own business. That's when I met Maria. *Thank you, universe.*

Maria is a neurotic, total control-otherwise-I-don't-sleep type of person. She is also completely no-nonsense and will tell you if you look fat, which I love about her. For example, her daughter had been dating a young man who liked to wine and dine her and she began to put on a little weight. No BS Maria rolls into the situation, "Look honey, you'd better be careful because he's gonna make you fat so no other man will want you." I can't help but chuckle cynically to a comment like that. Lacking a little tact? Yes. But it's totally honest, so you can't be a hater about it. Maria is one of the few people I know who will call out the elephant in the room that everyone is pretending to ignore without going through any internal dialogue or drama. She just does it.

Maria is also an inspiration. She came to America as a political refugee from Cuba escaping the clutches of Communism in the early 1960s. The only things she came to America with were her sister, mother, father and the clothing they had on their backs. No money. No home. Nothing.

She recalls her mother stuffing money and jewelry into her and her sister's coat pockets before the crossing, but her father tore the contents out of their pockets, yelling and spitting over his shoulder at Cuba. He wanted nothing from the communist regime. He swore that he and his family would make a life of freedom on their own without any benefit from anything communist. Maria was six years old.

When they landed in Miami, they had nowhere to go. They didn't speak English. They lived in a refugee camp comprised of tents and rations. Her father worked odd jobs to provide enough money to send Maria and her younger sister to school.

In all of my moments of fear, I cannot fathom the fear and helplessness that must have gripped Maria as she held her sister's hand outside that elementary school on their first day of classes as her sister looked up at her trembling with wide-eyes. How she didn't turn around and run away in tears escapes me, even now. Instead, Maria looked at her sister reassuringly, squeezed her little sister's hand, held her head up high, and marched right through those glass front doors.

Can't speak English? No problem. "Watch me learn," would be her response. Don't know anyone? No problem. "Watch me make friends." That is the type of person Maria is. She is the type of person that legends are made of, the type of person that historians dote upon. She is determined. She is brave.

Looking at this petite Cuban woman with red lipstick standing behind the counter at her clothing boutique just a few doors down from my shop, I never would have guessed either. Maria unwittingly unearthed her eMolecule when she was planning on playing a supporting role in a clothing boutique venture for her daughter. Well, the boutique didn't keep her daughter interested for very long, but it was too late for Maria to call it quits. She had just discovered her entrepreneurial self and couldn't go back to pre-eMolecule life.

She had recently retired from her position as a Probation Office for the U.S. Department of Justice. (I know, when you see her, you will never believe that this tiny little woman can kick some serious ass, but it's true.) The boutique kept her busy at first, but then Maria began to realize that she enjoyed the freedom to call all of the shots. I should also add that one of her favorite activities is shopping, and for those of you have never been shopping wholesale or at a trade show, you're missing out. It's like Costco on steroids and then some. I mean, why buy one pair of pants when you can buy twelve for the price of one?

Needless to say, Maria had found her element and her dream

job. She was in it for the hunt for new merchandise or better pricing and all of the negotiating and bargaining that goes along with purchasing from a wholesaler. One problem: Maria lacked the know-how and vision to run a business. Enter: Me, who was dealing with some serious self-doubt issues.

We quickly became friends. I helped her get her business in order. Excel spreadsheets are still a mystery to her, but her technology use as a whole has improved vastly. I also shared my story with her as we traveled to different tradeshows and events together. Not being a bullshitter, Maria predictably called me out point blank.

"You know what I think is wrong with you, Mary Elizabeth. You're scared. Life has dealt you some shit cards, but you're scared to do more." She always uses my middle name in these sorts of situations.

"Me? I'm not scared," as I totally lied through my teeth, which in case you are wondering is pointless when you're talking to a retired federal officer.

"Oh, please!" she exclaimed, calling my bluff. "I think you're afraid to do something else, something harder." Just like a mother, she chimes in, "Mary Elizabeth, you are so smart. You amaze me. You could do anything you want, but you sell sunglasses. You're a lawyer for chrissakes! AND YOU SELL SUNGLASS-ES!" Mom, don't worry, Maria's got your back.

I, wishing I could respond with something absolutely witty and intelligent, instead stammer, "Well, uh . . . er . . . I like sunglasses."

Then like a pro who has been coaxing the truth out of people for the last twenty years she throws in just enough of an ego inflator, "Amazing. You. Are. Am-A-Zing," emphasizing each syllable, "I don't know how you do it, but you're just amazing. I tell my husband that all the time. Amazing. Mary Elizabeth, you are amazing."

This is where I crumble completely, tell her she's right—because, of course, she is—I am scared, but I don't know what to do and then, with such wisdom and foresight, she proceeds to break down my entire sunglass store into the parts I like and don't like. And she is spot on. However, in true Mary fashion, I fail to put all of the pieces together and keep on keeping on, but at least I am getting closer to discovering my purpose. I can feel it.

XXV

BIRTHDAY WISHES OR REAL LIFE?

"There are three hundred and sixty-four days when you might get un-birthday presents, and only one for birthday presents, you know."

LEWIS CARROLL

So today is my birthday. No joke. (Well, it was the day I wrote this.) Every year, just like everyone else, I get one year older. I get to add another tally to the age number. Today, I wake up and see if I feel it yet: Am I a grown-up today? So far, nope. I still don't have all of the answers; I still don't know what I want to be when I grow up . . . whenever that happens. I know I'm getting closer, but I'm not quite there. I look in the mirror and feel pretty damn good about myself. "You go girl! Way to hold it together. You look pretty good for your age." I'm no 20-something, but I still pretend to rock a bikini and act like I am a 20-something in it. Whatever. I have fun and that's my point. I am finally proud to be me, and I *flaunt it!* Own up. The only person that can rock you is YOU. You are inimitable.

My best friend, Meghan, calls to wish me a "Happy Birthday." We start talking about birthdays and the expectations and goals that get set each year, which never seem to fully come to fruition. I look back on my life to date and recognize that it is absolutely 98 percent different than I imagined it would be by now. You know, when you're a kid and 30 is really old, your grandparents, only sixty-something or so, seem completely, unfathomably ancient. You draw on your ten-ish years of life experience to date and picture how your life will be: who you will become, where you will live, what your house will look like, your career. Well, mine is nothing like I imagined. I thought I would be single by choice—marriage, at least at the age of ten, was not something in the cards for me. I pictured I'd be living in a small, but smartly organized apartment in the middle of Any Big City, USA with two cats, and that every day I would don a smart business suit and go to my very important, well-paid career. Oh yeah, and I would be trilingual.

HA! That picture can't be further from the truth, except for the two cats part. I am married, can't imagine living in a city apartment again, and I despise professional attire (aptly named my "lawyer costume") in preference for flip-flops and leggings. Actually, no shoes at all are preferable, but I don't want to push it. Yes, to my husband's chagrin, I am part of the population that believes leggings constitute actual pants and that they're not tights. C'mon, they look like yoga pants, right? As far as my trilingual skills go, unless IKEA-nese and just-enough-Spanish-to-order-a-beer-in-Mexico count as two additional languages, I am sadly still monolingual.

I should add that if IKEA-nese doesn't count in your book, I might beg to differ. My fluency in IKEA's offerings and uncanny ability to piece together cohesive combinations from its various product lines has come in handy at least a half dozen times. Almost everything I own is from IKEA. Because I'm cheap? Maybe. Honestly, it's because first, we live really, really close to the coast and our house will most certainly flood in the event of a hurricane. As such, all of our fiberboard furniture will be super easy to replace. All we need is an Allen wrench, an AMEX, and a quick trip to IKEA. Second, if anything breaks/gets stained/ruined/or whatever, it was probably $35, so no skin off my back.

Back to my point: So as I was telling Meghan all of this, she interrupts to ask point blank. "So what?"

"What do you mean, so what?" I retort, a little offended.

"I mean, what would you change or do differently if you could go back and do it all over again?"

The answer: absolutely nothing. I would choose to do everything exactly the same because it is the culmination and aggregation of all the shit, the tears, the mistakes, the triumphs, the lessons, the love, the heartache, and the bumps along the way that have led me to where I am. I look around and actually like where I am. Is it perfect? Far from it, but I wouldn't change a thing. It is perfect in its imperfections. It's what gives me character. It is what makes me, well, *me*. If we were talking about houses, I believe real estate professionals dub this "charm." Yes, I have lots of "charm."

Coincidentally, this is the same day I texted her, "Megs, I am going to write a book."

XXVI

LIGHTNING STRIKES

"But how will I know it's my destiny?"
'Like love it will possess you... You can't help but know."

GAIL TSUKIYAMA,
The Street of a Thousand Blossoms

Have you ever had those moments when you walk into a room and you completely forget why you just walked in there? Well, now I'm talking about the moment that happens right after that. You know, when you leave the room and at some point down the hallway, the light bulb goes off, "Oh yeah! That's it!"

Okay, so we're on the same page now. Take that AHA! moment in the hallway and multiply it by one thousand. That is exactly how it hit me, the biggest, most overwhelming-it-almost-brought-me-to-tears moment standing right in my kitchen after finishing loading my newly installed and oh-so-quiet-when-it's-running dishwasher. I figured out what I wanted to do. *Nay. What I had to do.* It felt as if all of my experiences, learning, and self-exploration were in a blender for a very long time and then in the blink of an eye, the ingredients all formed together in unison to create one thing: *my purpose.*

Purpose for me is your path plus your passion. Or put differently, it's when your path and passion collide to forge a path, like a reverse fork in the road, two lanes merging into one wider, unified road. Maybe it even has lights on it. Mine does. And bear with me, it is the pursuit of our purpose that creates happiness and generates fulfillment. Our work doesn't make us happy, but rather our happiness guides us to want to do the work. Yes, those are some pearly white big ol' pearls of wisdom, so please, if you're good at Photoshop, feel free to put any of these pearly white quotes on a photo of me to post on Instagram or Pinterest. Actually, I'm just kidding. I think that is pretentious. You can't quote yourself. That's ridiculous!

Okay, seriously, let's talk about passion for a moment. It's elusive. Gurus or the like will tell you that you will find happiness if you do things in your life with passion. While I cannot disagree with this advice, I think the more pertinent issue we face is how do you find your passion? And no, the answer is not whatever makes you happy, because that creates a chicken and the egg sort of problem.

The answer is simpler, much, much simpler. It's what you *choose* to do with your free time or the thing that you jump up to do for a friend because you enjoy doing it, because it is rewarding. *That* is your passion. *That* is what your eMolecule is trying to tell you to do. Now, in my free time, yes, I have to choose to do things that I don't want to do, like vacuum, but I *have* to vacuum or suffer the consequences of being allergic to cats in a house full of cat fur. What I am talking about here is different. If you had zero obligations in the whole wide world and you needed nothing, how would you choose to spend your time?

If lying on the beach doing nothing is your answer, I have tried that, because I thought that would be my passion answer, but it actually gets boring after a little while. I know. Total bummer. Dig deeper. If you have no answer, that's okay too. I have planted a seed of awareness, if you remain aware of it and listen to what your heart and your body are telling you, you will find your answer soon enough. It will come to you if you choose to cultivate the seed.

Now, let's talk about the path because that is the second part of the equation to finding your purpose. Your path is essentially how you choose to practice your passion. My path is through entrepreneurship because I don't play well with others in a traditional organizational sense and because I like the freedom to change course without much ado.

However, there are some things that just aren't conducive to entrepreneurship. For example, if your passion is nursing and you are best served practicing in an emergency room, it may be more difficult to build a hospital and create an ER just so you can practice. However, you are, believe it or not, still harnessing the power of your eMolecule IF (and this is a big IF) you (1) consciously determined your passion and (2) consciously determined what path feeds your passion the most. Because if you have acknowledged both of these pieces, you are fulfilling your purpose the way it was meant for you and you are likely (and possibly unknowingly) providing feedback and creating innovation, even if just in small ways, so that you can better carry out your purpose, which is entrepreneurship in its most primal form. IF, however, you are hiding behind a job for its security, well I urge you to go back and re-read the section about the Cathys. You're an eMolecule faker and you are gypping yourself, which is not cool.

A former co-worker of mine, James, called me out of the blue one day and asked for my help. We set a time to meet up at a nearby Starbucks. He asked me about starting my sunglass store, and how I mustered up the courage to quit my job to do it.

"Wow, James. I guess I never thought of it as courage. I see it more as I didn't really have many options. I could choose to stay in my job and sacrifice my marriage or not. I couldn't risk losing Geoffrey, so I chose to quit my job. That's not courage. That's fear of losing your soul mate."

"No. That's courage." he responded firmly.

We continued discussing the startup process and different

corporate structures, pros, cons, accounting software, and planning minutiae until he asked, "So what is the biggest piece of advice you can give me?"

"I don't really give advice, James."

"Okay, so what's the worst thing or hardest thing about taking the plunge?"

"For me, the self-doubt. When I started, like most people just starting a new business, I was it: the only person. I simultaneously was marketer, sales clerk, planner, and buyer. It is isolating and breeds self-doubt because you're not only single-handedly coming up with the ideas, but you are also the only one okaying the ideas, and implementing them. There aren't a whole lot of checks and balances, so you doubt yourself along the entire way. That doubt can lead to inaction. Inaction leads to demise."

"So you were afraid?"

"Oh hell, yeah!"

"Really? You seem like you're never afraid. I can't believe this! So how do you get over the fear?"

"Well, again for me, I would cry in the corner and feel like a failure on Monday. On Tuesday, I would be upset at myself for wasting Monday, but still be afraid to take action. Wednesday, I would get over myself. Look myself in the mirror and yell at myself to stop wasting time. I mean, cakes don't bake themselves! *You* have to turn on the oven and *you* have to put them in to bake. Then, Thursday and Friday were always productive days."

"So how do I know if I can handle it?"

"First, you *will* be able to handle it. The universe doesn't throw things at you that you can't handle. Second, you will never know unless you start. And that means, no more prepping and planning. You have planned your business startup to the point of inaction. No matter how much planning you do, it will never be the perfect time to start and it will never be perfect on the first go. But if you don't start, you will never know."

Within two weeks of that meeting, James quit his job and followed his eMolecule. Fast forward into the future, he now owns and operates a very financially successful company and he can't even imagine his pre-eMolecule days. I asked him recently if he regretted harnessing his entrepreneurial spirit. His response, "Yes, I can't believe it took me so long."

And so standing in my kitchen, my nirvana of sorts had happened. It all fell into place and made sense. I reverse-engineered the "AHA!" in disbelief in my head.

"I love my eMolecule. I have always had a strong entrepreneurial spirit and prefer to pave my own way, even when it sucks or when it seems harder. Why have I kept ignoring it? I believe in myself. I am strong. My passions are educating others and business startup, both for myself and as an enabler for others. I love inspiring entrepreneurship."

"You did go to law school after all, Mary. You have a body of knowledge that not everyone has."

"But I want to help people. That feeds my soul."

"You can help people. First, you must tell people your story. You must be honest. Without honesty, there is no hope and no trust. You can inspire people with your story, but also give them the tools they need to grow and build a business."

"I can help people? . . . I can help people!"

"My purpose is to inspire entrepreneurship and share tools to facilitate those who don't have my legal knowledge or startup experience. I can help people find their eMolecules and discover their passions!"

It literally hit me, just like the moment I realized I was undeniably and eternally in love with my husband, Geoffrey. And just like love, there is absolutely nothing you can do about it. You can try to fight it, but you will lose. It might scare the hell out of you, but you can't help yourself from pursuing your purpose. It will keep you up at night with excitement and possibility. Will you still have moments of doubt? Yes, but you will overcome whatever obstacles present themselves. Remember, trust the universe and trust yourself.

I was reminded of this again when I was chatting with my mentor. After some conversation, he asked me about my book and whether it was done yet.

"No. I just . . . *was about to give you an excuse.*" I finished in my head.

"Let me tell you, it will take you one day to write your book." He stared at me unwaveringly. I stared back equally unwavering, but mine was in disbelief. "No, seriously," he continued, "let me ask you, will your book help people?"

"I hope so." I noncommittally responded.

"Wrong answer. You just told me you help people—that is your purpose. If your book doesn't help people, then why would you waste your time writing it? It would be meaningless without purpose"

"Yes. Yes it will help people." I affirmed with greater confidence.

"Then why isn't it done?" He pressed. I was about to open my mouth and fire off another see-through excuse before he chimed in, "Who are you to decide who you help or not? You don't get to choose. There are people out in the world who need your help, Mary, and they don't need it when you get around to it. They need it now. If someone needed your help right now, would you help them?"

"Of course." *That was a no-brainer,* I sighed in relief.

"Let me put this together for you, Mary. Your book will help people. There are people out there right this moment who need your help. Yet, you are depriving them of your help. Is that fair? No. Not to them. Not to you. So I urge you to stop preventing people from seeking the help they need. Every day you procrastinate is another day you deprive someone from getting help." And this is the part where I start crying. I cried because I was ashamed and guilty for forgetting my purpose—or at least for delaying the continued pursuit.

Just as my mentor urged me, I urge you to, if you know your purpose, harness your eMolecule and pursue it. It is the greatest gift to yourself because it is actually selfless. You have just now committed to giving your whole self to your purpose, and this is your gift to all of us. So go on. Go ahead, the world is waiting. . .

XXVII

THE POWER OF THREE

"Sometimes the slightest things change the directions of our lives, the merest breath of a circumstance, a random moment that connects like a meteorite striking the earth. Lives have swiveled and changed direction on the strength of a chance remark."

BRYCE COURTENAY

Three is a funny number, but it seems to have significant power in the universe—if you're into such aggrandizing statements. At least three seems to be popping up more in my life than ever before. To a certain extent, I have always lived my life by a rule of three. I tend to think that you should be willing to try out new things at least three times before passing the final verdict or disavowing something completely. Now, drawing from personal experience and just general goodwill, there are indeed things that shouldn't be tried once, let alone three times. These are of course things that intentionally harm you or others, and I think this can go without any further insight. So, why three, you ask?

Because the first time you try something, you don't know what to expect, so you aren't really educated enough to make a decision either way, but you inevitably show up with preconceived notions even with the best intentions about being open-minded.

The second time, you have a benchmark, so you can move your opinion either higher or lower. The third time, you know.

Take sushi, for example. The first time I tried sushi it was confusing. To be honest, I didn't *get* it. Why are people lining up like crazy to eat raw fish? However, applying my rule of three, I gave it another go. Okay, so this time I expected the texture, the bite of the wasabi. This isn't bad. It's pretty good actually. The third try: I *got* it. This isn't raw fish and rice—this is a delicate dance of balance, texture, flavor . . . this is art. *Tradition. Culture.* Wow. All of this in just one bite. Sushi is amazing!

Had I rendered final judgment after the first experience, I would not be a sushi-eater. Now, I'm not saying you are a loser if you don't eat sushi nor am I proclaiming that all must eat and love sushi. I'm just saying, if you don't give it a go—*a real go*—then you may be missing opportunities. In business, they get all heady and call it due diligence. Yeah, that too. You should do it. So maybe there really is truth in the old saying "third time's the charm."

In yoga, we are taught about balance. In fact, yoga is premised on the exploration, practice, and balance of the mind, body, and breath. Again, the theme of three appears.

A good friend and mentor, who has inspired me more than I will ever be able to share with him in words, bases his teachings on the awareness of three principles: grow, give, and gratitude. If you are not feeling fulfilled, then there is imbalance in one of these areas of your life. Or conversely, when you are aware of and align your *three* Gs, you will find happiness and fulfillment.

I had the opportunity to listen in on a presentation by another thought leader of our times, who also preached the power of three in his holistic success model. In his message, he defines success as a balance between relationships, finances, and health. When you forgo or sacrifice one of these areas in pursuit of the others, you will not succeed.

In cooking, regardless of culture or region, a foundation of three ingredients lays down the success and flavor of a recipe.

The French use the mirepoix, or a combination of onions, celery, and carrot. Cajun cooking uses the Holy Trinity: onions, bell pepper, and celery. Spanish, Portuguese, and Latin American cuisines are heavily based on sofrito—three base ingredients varying by region that define the food from that specific geographic area. Asian food culture is similarly based on the foundation of garlic, ginger, and green onion.

Why is there so much emphasis on the unity of three? Perhaps this is due to the strength of the triangle. The triangle in physics, math, and architecture is the most stable and strongest shape. The triangle doesn't easily deform and is the only basic geometric shape able to sustain balance despite stretching and compressive forces from inside or outside its structure. It is the go-to shape for bridge trusses, buildings, and even bicycle frames. The Egyptians iconically used a three dimensional form of a triangle, the pyramid. Enough said, right?

Well, how about this: a triangle is the only shape that is "perfect." An equilateral triangle is called a perfect triangle, yet when a rectangle has four sides of equal length, it is not called a perfect rectangle, but rather a square. Then, there is the common misnomer of a "perfect" circle. A circle is by its definition a "perfectly" round shape, but it is just called a circle. Any distortion to its circumference and the circle morphs into an oval or ellipse. Thus, only the triangle, with its three sides is every really recognized as being perfect.

Beyond the purely "physical" properties there lies a more powerful internal meaning. The number three symbolizes a harmony that comes from integrating two opposites. One, like a circle, is the symbol for unity. There is obvious agreement that when something exists on its own, there is nothing to create disturbance. Two, on the other hand, symbolizes tension and complexity. Then, three comes along and merges one and two to create a new harmonious entity that includes unity plus peace and tension plus discord. Without unity and tension, three could not exist. A triangle would not stay held together. A triad would be impossible.

My take on this is simple. The number three or a triangle or any other iteration of three holds within it chaos, peace, disagreement, and unity, basically all of the super ugly stuff we try to avoid, as well as all of the beautiful, breathtaking moments of our human experience. This humble thing, three or a triangle, is able to withstand all of these powerful forces coming at it from the outside world and the inside world within you and, yet, we call it perfect.

It would seem that the number three, then, has indeed intentionally impacted my life. Even though I live by my own rule of three, practice yoga, cook every day, and heed the words and advice from my friends and mentors, there are three things that were truly needed for me to harness my eMolecule, so I guess you could call these three things my holy trinity of sorts.

One. Choosing to overcome fear and self-doubt. This is honestly just a choice. You can choose to get over it or choose to succumb. I know that I will never be able to fully silence those nagging voices of irrationality, but I can control them. Yes, they still creep up, but I have the power, as we all do, to step back and not let them take the reins. This is the hardest part. Honestly.

•

Two. Pick a Direction, even if the destination is still unknown. Most of the time, I don't know where I am going, but I know my path will lead me to the destination that is right for me. Don't ask why or how. Just have faith that everything you truly need will be available when you need it. This isn't easy either, but, gosh, is it rewarding! Opportunities will arise that would go unnoticed if you were to remain closed off to their possibility. Yes, you will stray from your path and your direction, but you will always find your way back onto it if you have faith.

•

Three. You must act. Just start. It doesn't have to matter. It doesn't have to be perfect. It doesn't have to be the full dream. Just start. If you never start, you will never know what you are capable of. You will never find yourself fulfilled. Mere existence without meaning does not show respect and gratitude for this thing called life and it is a sacred gift not meant to be squandered. You must act.

•

EPILOGUE

I, again, found myself faced with a profound decision to make. Instead of playing it safe like a Chicago Cubs fan and proclaiming, "there's always next year," I definitively and irrevocably made my choice. I decided to overcome my fear in this moment. I knew this opportunity would not present itself again, and I took action. I rose from my seat and readied to take the stage. I didn't even know what I was going to say, but I had one hundred steps to figure it out . . .

ACKNOWLEDGEMENTS

So many individuals have left an impression on me. Some have changed the way I think, some the way I act, but all have changed my life.

I would like to take a moment and give special thanks to a few of the individuals that have been instrumental:

To Anil. I asked the universe for a helper, and the universe sent me to you. I couldn't have imagined a better helper. You recognized the possibility I held within and waited patiently for me to come into self-realization of it. I had the seed, but you showed me that I also had the water to nurture it. You saw the real me and held me accountable. You shared your gift with me; you held up the mirror so I could see myself. Thank you. Thank you. Thank you.

To Kytka, at Distinct Press. Without your faith in my vision, this book may have never happened. Thank you for your direction and guidance throughout this process. You are a master of your craft with an ability to see hidden potential. I speak comfortably in my voice now and stand confidently that I know it is mine. Thank you for this opportunity. I have a feeling that this is just the beginning.

To my "sandwich neighbor" and dear friend, Dachelle. Thank you for bridging the gap between Geoffrey and me when we needed a neutral ground to meet on. You will always be my go-to partner in crime anytime I need anything over-the-top. Your ridiculous stories and encounters always keep me laughing and smiling.

To Dr. Mark Hoelscher, who showed me (and everyone else in his classes) that life is indeed what you make of it: the good, the bad, and the super nasty ugly parts. Your candid stories of how you ended up where you're at proves that success is truly defined by family, relationships, love, and compassion, not money. More importantly, you taught me that I could be anything I wanted to be . . . and gave it a name: entrepreneurship. If only I had heeded your advice sooner and been brave enough to look inside and trust my entrepreneurial spirit, I could have saved a bundle on student loans! I will always be your student, so please keep inspiring those around you to take the path less travelled.

To Maria, a stranger turned dear friend, who saw my light and believed in me when I had little faith in myself and my abilities. You unknowingly helped me get back onto my path and recognized my true passion before I did. Without your confidence in me coupled with your inability to use technology, I may never have had my "I finally figured out what I want to be when I grow up" AHA! moment. Over the course of our joint ventures and personal friendship spanning many miles of Florida highway, you listened generously as I shared my story with you. You encouraged me to share my story with others. So, dear reader, you can thank her if my story speaks to you.

To the loving community and leaders at Bala Vinyasa Yoga / Green Monkey. Kiersten, your radiance, energy, and vision inspired me to consider possibility in my own life. You lead by example and I am humbled by your generosity and strength. Hanna, thank you for helping me take the first steps in my yoga practice. Your shining spirit and attitude provided a light for me to follow when I wasn't sure if I had a light of my own. Candice, thank you for making it worth my while to peel myself out of sweet dreams at dawn in order to find solace on my mat. Angela, you are the overseer and caretaker of our beautiful sanctuary. Though not glamorous, it is noble and important; we are grateful for you. Kim, thank you for standing witness to my transformation, teaching me, and encouraging me to keep on keepin' on.

To my girls, the Miracle Makers, Erin, Cynde, Sue, Jami, Sophie, Leslie, Kimberly, Jenn, Paige, Joanie, Bianca, Allie, Abby, Jenny, Chloe, and Irmela. Thank you for holding space for me and listening generously. I acknowledge each and every one of you for courageously sharing your stories, lives, fears, hopes, joys, and dreams. You have taught me so many lessons and inspire me to continue the work I have started. Please keep sharing with me; I'm listening.

To my best friend, Meghan, who has been closer than a sister to me in good times and bad. Your attitude and gumption inspire me to be a better person every day. You are amazing. I cannot tell you how much you have impacted my life. You were the first person, besides Geoffrey, that I told about failing the bar exam. You helped give me the courage to pick myself back up and reassured me that the worst that could happen is that I would fail again, which "is no biggie! You got this Mar!" Maybe in my next life, I will be more like you. Thank you, Meghan, from the bottom of my heart.

To my sister, Sarah. I know why I have to fight so hard for your trust and love. Please forgive me.

To Dad. Without you, well, I wouldn't be an Alabama Crimson Tide fan or such a huge football fan, and, gosh, I can't imagine a fall without football! But more importantly without you, I wouldn't have developed my inquisitive mind and developed (my still learning) skill of patience. You've showed me hard work and perseverance and how to be a compassionate leader. Thank you for always reading Dr. Seuss's *Bartholomew and the Oobleck* to me whenever requested at bedtime, despite it being one of the longest children's books ever; always coloring with me, putting together a puzzle, or letting me tinker alongside you in the yard or garage. Thank you for helping me recognize the qualities and traits for my perfect match and partner in life: you lead by example. And of course, you taught me about sailing and incubated a love for the ocean. I am forever grateful and think of you every time we set sail into the sunset. I love you so much.

To Mom. It goes without saying that I hold such admiration and love for you. Folks, the apple doesn't fall far from the tree on this one. Mom, you once asked me where I got my leadership skills and moxy. Well, let's just say those traits are carefully cultivated and nurtured by their creator. If you look in the mirror, you will see where I get it. You are so strong and skilled, eloquent and intelligent. You have taught me so much through your words but profoundly through your actions. I want nothing more than to make you proud. You can finally rest. I am living my dream and sharing it with my soul mate . . . everything you ever wanted for your daughter. Your journey, its love and sacrifice, has not been forsaken. I love you.

And to the most instrumental of them all, my husband and soul mate, Geoffrey, whose undying love, unwavering support, complete selflessness, and seemingly irrational belief that I would make a difference in the world has made this entire journey possible. I love you more than I can elementarily express with words. I live each and every day grateful for you and for everything you've made possible. Thank you for standing in true partnership with me as we create our future together. And I have a secret to share: our future is going to be more than we ever dreamt possible. I can feel it!

ABOUT THE AUTHOR

Mary Todd is anything but ordinary. She can be described as an entrepreneur, author, speaker, yoga teacher, attorney, and adventurer, but is defined by no single title. She is a true visionary that will lead the next generation of thought leaders and action takers.

Her passion is entrepreneurship and her purpose is to share her story and what she knows to inspire greatness in others by helping them find their eMolecules and empowering them with the tools to create, build and grow a successful business centered on their passions.

She strongly holds to the creed that anyone can change the world if willing to do the work to step into greatness by showing up each and every day with courage and compassion. She has founded countless businesses, both brick and mortar and online, but is most proud of her work inspiring and educating entrepreneurs.

You can learn more about what Mary is up to and stay up to date on her adventures at:

www.eMaryTodd.com

WHAT'S NEXT

Are you ready to harness
your entrepreneurial spirit today?

Get instant free access to the
"5 Strategies to Ignite Your eMolecule Now!"

www.eMaryTodd.com/free-gift